CONCILIUM

Religion in the Eighties

CONCILIUM

Concilium 187 (5/1986): Third World Theology

CONCILIUM

OPTION FOR THE POOR: CHALLENGE TO THE RICH COUNTRIES

Edited by
Leonardo Boff
and
Virgil Elizondo

English Language Editor
Marcus Lefébure

T. & T. CLARK LTD
Edinburgh

October 1986
T. & T. Clark Ltd, 59 George Street, Edinburgh EH2 2LQ
ISBN: 0 567 30067 6

ISSN: 0010-5236

Typeset by Print Origination Formby Liverpool
Printed by Page Brothers (Norwich) Ltd

Concilium: Published February, April, June, August, October, December.
Subscriptions 1986: UK: £19.95 (including postage and packing); USA: US$40.00
(including air mail postage and packing); Canada: Canadian $50.00 (including air
mail postage and packing); other countries: £19.95 (including postage and
packing).

CONTENTS

EDITORIAL: THEOLOGY FROM THE VIEWPOINT OF THE POOR

THE PREFERENTIAL option for the poor is the trademark of the Latin American church. Today, however, it is becoming an option of the universal Church. John XXIII, on 11 September 1962, when he announced the Second Vatican Council, gave it a clear direction, a reference point for a whole understanding of the Church: 'The Church is and wishes to be the Church of all, but principally the Church of the poor.' John Paul II has repeated times without number that 'the option for the poor is my daily concern'. In *Laborem Exercens* he says that in showing solidarity with exploited workers the Church proves its fidelity to Christ and becomes 'truly the Church of the poor' (para 8).

The preferential option for solidarity with the poor is nothing short of a Copernican revolution for the Church. The protagonist in history and society who henceforth implements the Christian mission will be the poor. Through the poor all others are summoned and drawn, but it is to be the poor who are the privileged bearers of the message.

What are the implications of the option for the poor, as made by the new churches of the periphery or by the central churches of the great tradition? It implies a genuine conversion, which includes a number of elements we wish to highlight. The option for the poor requires:

(1) *a vision of the reality of the poor through the eyes of the poor.* We usually see the poor through the eyes of the rich, and so the poor appear as

those without possessions, without knowledge, without power. They are those in want, the object of help from those with power, knowledge and possessions. When we enter the continent of the poor and try to think through their eyes and from their social position, we discover their strength, their resistance, their courage and their creativity. It then becomes clear that the society within which they live and suffer and from which they are marginalised has to be fundamentally transformed. From the position of the poor the urgency of liberation is beyond doubt.

The option for the poor demands:

(2) *that we take up the cause of the poor*. The cause of the poor is the cause of life and the means of life such as work, bread, clothing, housing and basic education. The cause of the poor is a new society in which the vital questions which concern all citizens without distinction are given priority, in which relations of collaboration and equity prevail over exploitation and domination. The Christian churches can make an invaluable contribution to the planning and building of a society centred more on persons and meeting their needs than on increasing the pace of development and accumulation.

The option for the poor implies:

(3) *that we take up the struggle of the poor*. It is the oppressed who bring about liberation. They become aware of their dignity, organise their action, form links with other groups which, like them, want a different society. The churches should join this struggle, make their specific contribution as religious bodies, reinforce the power of the poor to enable them to press for changes and participate in their implementation. It is not for the churches to produce a parallel programme unconnected with that of the oppressed. In *Latin America* the urgent question (though of course there are other important ones) is political and social liberation, because it is in this area that there exist the major injustices, which amount to a social sin. The churches must insert this urgent dimension within an overall perspective of the full salvation won by Christ. In *Africa* the urgent question is that of culture threatened with destruction by a Western attitude based on knowledge as domination and production for consumption. The Christian churches cannot appear as channels for neo-colonialism by transmitting the Christian message in European cultural dress. Africanisation of the church, of theology and liturgy is a form of support to African identity. In *Asia* the most pressing challenge is constituted by religions which are historically more ancient than Christianity. How are we to interpret them theologically, and how can we ensure that they too become promoters of justice and of the humanisation of the oppressed? The task for the churches is to overcome their almost automatic suspicion of the new forms of liberation which correspond to equally profound forms of

oppression such as those suffered by women, Blacks, ethnic minorities and the new poor (drug dependents, marginalised homosexuals, neglected old people and the unemployed), and to give positive support to the efforts of all those who are trying to widen the space of their freedom.

The option for the poor includes yet another aspect:

(4) *taking up the life of the poor*. The option for the poor is not authentic unless we participate, at least a little, in the life and sufferings of the poor. In view of the world crisis and the crisis in the sense of solidarity, there is an obligation on all to adopt an anti-consumerist attitude, more simple and ecological. Support for the struggles of the poor frequently means suffering misunderstanding, persecution and even moral and physical injury. Many people have been imprisoned, tortured and even killed by those who oppose all change. In the first world Christians and theologians who take up prophetic positions stemming from the option for the poor are discriminated against and suffer even at the hands of fellow members of the household of the faith. Such sad occurrences should not embitter those who feel united to the poor. On the contrary, they should feel solidarity as they share the heavy lot imposed on the oppressed.

The option for the poor in the first and third worlds demands further:

(5) *identification of the mechanisms which produce poverty*. Much has already been written about the 'source of the wealth of the poor'. Today we need to be clear about 'the source of the poverty of the poor'. The poverty of the poor is a result of a combination of causes, and first the international capitalist system and the *relations of dependence and oppression* it establishes between the nations at the centre of the system and those at the periphery. This is particularly true of Western countries. We live within a single system of production, but the benefits and costs are unequally distributed. The benefits are, on the whole, accumulated by the countries which are already highly developed or by the social classes in the poor countries which exercise social control in association with the multi-national interests of capital. The sacrifices are borne by those who are already poor and exploited. Development and underdevelopment are linked by a causal connection which makes them two sides of the same coin. If the churches and the theologians do not develop a critical attitude towards the socio-economic system within which they live, they run the risk of becoming mere reformists, reproducing the system in a slightly improved form, rather than allies of the poor, who are demanding a once-for-all replacement of the existing system by another which makes possible more equality and life for all.

Finally, the option for the poor implies:

(6) *a redefinition of the task of theology*. Theology's mission is to produce

light and rational understanding in relation to the Christian mystery. But it must also evangelise, that is, produce the good news. It evangelises by also being prophetic, denouncing specific oppressions and announcing God's plan in history. It evangelises by being pastoral and inspiring a commitment to liberation. A theology today which does not place at the centre of its concerns the poor, justice, freedom and liberation will have difficulty in refuting the accusation of alienation and even cynicism, and will in the end become totally irrelevant. The credibility of the churches and of Christian thought is now being measured by the way in which they face the question of the poor. We must never forget that the poor are, in the last resort, our eschatological judges. Without the poor the church loses its Lord and theology its evangelical content. Because of the union between Christ and the poor we can understand the words of Georges Bernanos, which could well be the motto of this whole issue of *Concilium*:

I tell you, it is the poor who will save the world. They will save it without meaning to. They will save it in spite of themselves. They will not ask anything in return for this, simply through not knowing the value of the service they have performed.

[*Les enfants humiliés*, Paris 1949, p. 219]

Translated by Francis McDonagh   Virgil Elizondo
                                                         Leonardo Boff

Part I

The Reality of Wealth at the Cost of Poverty

Julio de Santa Ana

How the Rich Nations came to be Rich

IN MARCH 1967, Paul VI produced his encyclical *Populorum Progressio*, which was generally greeted with the enthusiasm accorded only to messages that manage to encapsulate the expectations of large sectors of humanity. *This document echoed the hopes* of those who were looking for substantial changes in the relations between developed and underdeveloped countries. Through processes of sustained economic growth, developing countries would be able, in a relatively short space of time, to achieve levels of production, consumption and distribution of goods that would enable them to combat poverty and all that stems from it. Paul VI's text was redolent of the spirit of an age: the age of the first decade of development launched by the United Nations, during which conditions for 'peaceful co-existence' between the Superpowers who seek to control the lives of all nations on this planet were also being worked out.

Less than twenty years later, we find ourselves in a very different situation from that in which *Populorum Progressio* saw the light of day. Many of the 'hopes' of those days have been shown to be little more than *illusions*. One only needs to study the change in terminology employed by those concerned with questions relating to development to see at once that the optimism of those times has become a cautious exercise tinged with deep pessimism. To take just one example: during the sixties, hardly anyone spoke about the situation of the poor. Poverty seemed simply something that was inevitably about to be eradicated. Everything pointed in this direction, sooner or later. And yet today it seems that poverty, rather than diminishing, has grown. Since the mid-seventies we have talking about the relationship between 'rich nations and poor nations', and at about the same time the term 'fourth world' was coined to denote pockets of poverty in the midst of the overall plenty of the rich nations. Then came the distinction between 'developing countries' and 'less developed countries', the latter term denoting those countries whose economic indicators did not provide any evidence of ability to overcome the harsh reality of the poverty extant in them.

This shows at least three things. First, that when estimates and plans were drawn up in the sixties showing that poverty and hunger could be eliminated from the world, conditions were such as to allow such assumptions to be made. These were based on estimates of world production, growth in productive output and the needs of the population of the planet. The problem could be resolved through certain adjustments to the structures of world trade. The 'development of nations' was, therefore, a viable prospect. Second, this error in perspective was related to an inadequate understanding of the durability of structures that had been built up over long periods and showed extreme resistance and lack of flexibility in the face of proposed changes through international treaties and agreements. This meant therefore, thirdly, that the poverty of nations and their underdevelopment is intimately connected with the way in which economic and political power is structured and the manner in which it is exercised. Trying to understand this situation adequately involves taking a *historic and dynamic view* that takes account of social and productive relationships within nations and between them.

1. THE RELATIONSHIP BETWEEN DOMINATION AND ECONOMIC GROWTH

A leading Brazilian economist, Celso Furtado, has stated that 'Two basic forms of appropriation of surplus value seem to have existed since the dawn of history. On one hand is what we might call the *authoritarian form*, which consists in extracting surplus through coercion. On the other is the *mercantile form*, or acquisition of surplus through the framework of the means of trade and exchange.' In this way, simply and directly, Furtado sets us within the historical process that allows us to understand the conditions that allowed some nations to grow economically at the expense of others. This is especially applicable to those nations that began the production cycle we now know as capitalism.[1]

The *authoritarian form* appears in history when one nation or social group comes to dominate or subjugate another. But it also comes about through control of productive land or water and energy supplies, or through the imposition of taxes from positions of strength. The *mercantile form*, on the other hand, is found not simply in the processes of trade, but particularly related to a process of expanding productivity. Those who control the means of production and exchange (and the two are generally closely connected) then come to take possession of the surplus that comes from population growth.

It needs to be pointed out that, in general, societies breeding in normal human conditions (that is, when not affected by natural catastrophes such as drought, earthquake and flood, or man-made ones such as war and its social consequences), not only tend to assure their life support through production, but also *always* to increase in numbers. This growth in numbers and the conditions which allow it to be maintained produce the surplus. Acquisition of this surplus has been the principal motive behind conquests, crusades and wars, as it is now behind the drive to control markets.

Once one sees that the *process of accumulation is linked in this way to conquest and market dominance*, one can then understand how certain nations have been able to build up the economic power they possess today. In other words, it is clear that the economic growth of Western nations has depended largely on their colonial empires, to the sack of which those countries now called underdeveloped and poor were put. It is not that those nations seen as industrially developed today have managed to formulate rational modes of work and production, in which the discipline of the workforce is a basic component in the achievement of high productivity. It is rather that a high level of output cannot be achieved simply through hard work: it requires other conditions, among which accumulation of capital ranks highest.[2] It was just this accumulation of surplus through a combination of conquest, colonial expansion and market control on a world scale that provided the conditions for the ability to take a great leap forward in capitalist production with the industrial revolution.

This shows that the process of accumulating wealth does not depend on purely economic factors: it also involves elements of great political import. This is why I am saying that the build-up of wealth and power by those nations that have reached the highest levels of economic growth was generally based on a course of domination which, while generating wellbeing for the conquering country, produced the poverty of the conquered. So we have to say that *development and underdevelopment are two faces of the same coin*.

But the problem does not end within these parameters. Colonial exploitation did not just mean riches for some and death and poverty for others. It unleashed an *unbridled desire for oppression* on the part of the conquerors over the conquered. For example, in Latin America, the arrival of the Spaniards produced a profound subversion of the indigenous order that had lasted till then in those lands. Of course, the organisation of the Indian societies also involved injustices, but nothing to be compared with the violent domination imposed by the Spanish and Portuguese. Through the system of 'concessions', *conquistadores* came to administer vast tracts of land and their inhabitants. Their objective was to reach the highest possible level of production on these lands, without regard for the means of achieving it, nor the consequences for the people. The result was the virtual extermination of the population. Natives were obliged to work beyond their strength, which diminished their resistance to disease. So a few decades saw *virtual genocide* in the regions of Mexico and Central America. For every ten Indians living when the Spanish arrived, hardly one was still alive sixty or seventy years later.

Faced with the situation of no longer having cheap local labour, the colonizers resorted to the *importation of slave labour*. The slave trade already existed, but from the sixteenth to the early nineteenth centuries, routes were set up which were continually plied by ships loaded with men and women from the coasts of Angola, Dahomey and other parts of Africa, bound for the colonies established by various European countries in the Americas. This 'negro traffic' was one of the vilest forms of human exploitation known to history. No one knows precisely how many Africans were taken to America under these conditions. But by examining statistics from the various colonies, and bearing in mind the fact that many died on the way, owing to the appalling conditions they were forced to undergo in the holds of the ships, it is possible to arrive at a figure of tens of millions.

The *working conditions* imposed on them on reaching America were equally dreadful. The slave traffic that began in the sixteenth century with its implacable exploitation of black muscle-power also began discrimination against Blacks. From then on, the existence of Black people cannot be seen apart from capitalism and productive processes. They were seen basically as a source of labour and profit. Just as the Indians were dragged off to work and lose their lives in the mines, so the Negroes were forced to give their lives to enrich those of colonials grasping at fame and fortune. This is how social stratification in America began, and even now, in both North and South America, the two groups most visibly deprived of opportunity are the Indians and the Blacks. This legacy from the colonial past is indelibly impressed on most societies of the American hemisphere.

Historically, colonial domination was a constant necessity for those nations that sought political and commercial dominance. Without the products obtained at very low cost in their colonies, they would never have been able to improve living conditions in their own lands. Nor, more importantly, would they have been able to create the conditions in which to expand their own industries. This of course was not sufficient in itself. They also had to eliminate possible competitors, which meant preventing their industrialisation. This they did through the application of violent means aimed at destroying local centres of production. Once the dominating nations had gained control of trade, they could impose their own products on colonial markets. This sort of control had clear cultural consequences that can still be seen today: 'The rapid expansion of trade was triggered by the advances in productivity made in areas to which capitalism spread. The new products made possible by changing production processes spearheaded new trade routes. This contact between one culture vowed to innovation and expansion and others still attached to tradition produced a situation in which the former came to dominate the latter, since these tended to *aspire* to reproducing the consumer models of the former. There can be many explanations of this process, but they must all take account of the fact that the culture that first came to depend on the capitalist means of production was based on a quicker process of accumulation, which meant *inter alia* that it could impose trade and its products on others by force. So, to sum up: the formation of a process of international division of labour was not just a matter of opening up new trading patterns; it was also, and mainly, one of imposing new cultural patterns.'[3]

The destruction of local industries in the colonised nations forced them to become *suppliers of raw materials for the 'mother' countries*. This resulted in their impoverishment. This impoverishment was nevertheless also the lot of most of the workers in the colonial powers. Though their situation began to improve at the end of the nineteenth century, it should not be forgotten that several European nations were in states of serious crisis at the time of the Great War, which became worse during the great depression years of 1928-32, when the workers and peasants of Europe and North America came to know the pains of sinking back into conditions of severe poverty. We should not forget, all the same, that the worst sufferers were the countries of Africa, Latin America and Asia.

The crisis of capitalism during the last years of the twenties and the beginning of the thirties was a decisive factor in bringing about the World War of 1939-45. The means taken to overcome the crisis were, in effect, contributory factors to the greatest conflict humanity has ever seen. This led statisticians and economists, who saw that corrections introduced into the world economy were inadequate to restore the equilibrium lost in this conflict, to assert the need to create a *new international economic order*. The foundations for this were first put forward at the Bretton Woods Conference of 1944, shortly before the end of the World War. Unfortunately, the Bretton Woods order has not helped to resolve the problem of poverty. If anything, it has made it worse.

2. THE PRESENT INTERNATIONAL ORDER

One has to recognise the magnitude of the task facing those who met at

Bretton Woods. Witnesses to a huge catastrophe, and seeking to prevent it from ever happening again, they worked out conditions that would lead to the stabilisation of world trade and the markets through which it operates. So they postulated a *series of conditions under which humanity could return to a peaceful existence.* Among these was the creation of a vast international market-place which would promote the existence of *free trade*, without protectionist barriers to impede its development. Free trade means a *free market*, which at the same time implies the existence of *free exchange.* This meant doing away with competing areas in which production ran the risk of being swamped, without a market outlet, as had happened in the years leading up to 1928. The aim was to avoid the maintenance of parallel trading areas: the dollar area, the sterling area, the franc area, etc. What Bretton Woods brought about was the creation of a huge, strong 'free trade' system. This meant a return (with adjustments suitable to the twentieth century) to the *economic theories of Adam Smith.* However, the Western powers who by one means or another played the most influential role at the Conference, were not completely at one in accepting these principles. In effect, what emerged was, in the words of the Report of the Brandt Commission, 'a combination of Keynes for home affairs, and Adam Smith overseas.[5]

To safeguard the development of this economic order, two institutions were set up which still play a preponderant role in the course of world economic affairs. These are the *International Bank for Reconstruction and Development*, generally known as the World Bank, and the *International Monetary Fund* (IMF). Through their operations, they have gradually succeeded in bringing most countries in the world (including some socialist ones) within the framework of the system set up at Bretton Woods. Only fifty countries were at that meeting, but now more than 120 are involved with the World Bank and the IMF. This evolution was due to the needs of the 'Third World' countries for economic growth, and those of the newly independent nations resulting from the de-colonisation process of the fifties and sixties. All these countries have been in need of international credit at one time or another. They appealed for this to the World Bank, which was only too willing to open up avenues of credit if the countries asking for it *demonstrated their willingness to run their economies according to the lines laid down at Bretton Woods.* The verdict on this is given by the IMF, which contacts the countries asking for money and suggests measures which will gradually bring them within the framework of the system. The famous 'letters of intent' are what give concrete form to acceptance of the great system of international free trade by countries which, from that time on, agree to run their economies according to the guidelines produced by the World Bank and the IMF.

Those who met at Bretton Woods in 1944 came from the countries within the *capitalist orbit*. The Soviet Union had abstained. And though it is true that a certain number of socialist countries (Rumania, Hungary, China, etc.) have since come into the system, there is no doubt that the general orientation of the agreements follows the lines of the development of world capitalism. This development, since 1945, has certainly been impressive. Never in world history has there been such a period of expansion as the last forty years. Never has there been such economic growth as has been concentrated into the past four decades. But at the same time, never has there been such a degree of concentration of wealth into few hands, while the poverty of the majority increased. The guidelines laid down by the Bretton Woods Conference have produced a *particular evolution of capitalism*, which has been described as a 'process of internationalising capital and the workforce'. This not only means an accelerated process of capital expansion on a world scale, but has also brought into being the principal instrument of this expansion in the shape of the new and powerful economic agencies of the multi-national corporations. The world expanison of capital—the rapid growth of foreign capital in the underdeveloped countries—has been accompanied by the international concentration and centralisation of capital. This concentration and centralisation operate on a horizontal plane (a single economic sector), a vertical plane (from raw material to finished product) and in cross-section.

'The international concentration and centralisation of capital have created a new agency in the process of uneven development: the multi-national corporation, that form of individual capital multiplied on a world scale. This is the phase of real, no longer merely formal, creation of a *world market*—the market for consumer goods, capital and labour. At the same time, international division of labour has become the function of a personnel department within the corporation . . . For internationally concentrated and centralised capital, the world has become a single continuum, not only for the sale of goods but also for purchase of the means of production.'[5]

Through the operations of *transnational capital*, whose origin and greatest strength is just in the industrially developed countries of the North, the process of appropriating the surplus produced by the countries of the South has been accentuated by those who control the capitalist production system. In this way, the increased production of the underdeveloped countries, though it has been dramatic over the last forty years, has not substantially aided their development. So we find paradoxical situations such as that in Africa, where food production has reached record levels, yet most countries on that continent are today facing problems of hunger, from which they have generally been free in the past.

The impoverishment of the South has gone hand in hand with an increase in the wealth of the North. For probably the first time in history, most of the population of Europe, Japan and the United States have moved beyond poverty into conditions of great abundance. This can be seen from a comparision between access to consumer goods in the countries of the North and those of the South. Back in 1972 Rudolf Strahm showed that the annual consumption per head in Switzerland was equal to that of twenty-three people in India or forty in Somalia.[6] An even more impressive statistic is that the United States, with 6% of the world's population, consumes almost 40% of the world's produce. This inequality in the distribution of goods is the best indicator that the *international economic order agreed at Bretton Woods is incapable of eradicating poverty from our societies.* While it may have helped to do so in the Northern hemisphere, it has unfortunately made conditions worse in the Southern.

3.   THE INJUSTICE OF INTERNATIONAL TRADE

As I said at the beginning of this article, the *climate prevailing twenty years ago was one of general optimism.* Of course it was also seen that the world situation was difficult. But there was not the same realisation as we have today of the obstacles standing in the way of changing this situation. I have already mentioned the encyclical *Populorum Progressio* in this context. There was also the Report of the 'World Conference on Church and Society', organised by the WCC in Geneva in 1966, which shared the same view. Outside the Church sphere, this optimism seemed even more pronounced. Suffice to remember that the United Nations launched the 'First Decade of Development' in the sixties. During this decade, many regional economic conferences were held, culminating in the 'World Conference on Commerce and Development', which took place in Geneva from March to May 1964. It was then thought that programmes organised and supervised by the international community could contribute to the gradual eradication of poverty and hunger. One of the most important means for achieving this was to be *international aid.* This led to the creation of UNCTAD, understood as an 'organization charged with carrying on negotiations and deciding courses of action,[7]

Unfortunately, events combined to show that *these hopes were far from being realised.* It was soon seen that international aid was proving less abundant than had been hoped, let alone generous. UNCTAD found it difficult to produce deals that would help the countries that exported *raw materials.* These countries then began to form themselves into a *bloc* that would serve as a framework for putting their wishes into effect. Meeting in Algeria in 1965, they worked out a document which stated that they had reached 'the clear understanding that any genuine efforts aimed at development should start with them. Only on the basis of their own internal efforts would they be able to play a constructive role in working out mutually beneficial international policies,[8]

This meant that by the mid-sixties it was becoming clear to the countries of *Africa, Asia and Latin America* that their struggle against the conditions that engendered poverty had to be carried on through *creating a new situation* in which they would be able to achieve sustained development. Unfortunately, they were unable to bring this about. The fact is that if they were to generate conditions of this sort, it was essential for their raw materials to hold their value. What actually came about was a situation of 'deteriorating terms of trade'.

The process that worked against the interests of those countries whose basic produce is raw materials came about—and is still coming about—in two ways. First, the *price of raw materials has not held up* compared to the price of finished goods from the industrialised countries. For example, in Burma in 1960, four tons of rubber had to be produced to buy a jeep. Ten years later, the cost of a jeep was the equivalent of ten tons of rubber. This tendency, as Paul Presbisch, first secretary-general of UNCTAD, has shown, has been going on since the end of the last century. This means that the underdeveloped countries constantly have to produce more in order to be able to go on importing the same quantity of manufactured goods, which is the same as saying that there has been a continuous fall in the purchasing power of the underdeveloped countries.[9]

Second, this deterioration in the terms of trade is brought about on another level too, taking account of the fact that not only do prices of raw materials go down in relation to prices of manufactured goods from the highly industrialised nations, but also the *volume of trade* thereby benefits the latter and penalises the former. This can be seen by comparing the increase in the developed countries' trading figures compared to those of the countries that produce raw materials: 'the balance of exchange between the two groups of countries has shifted against the Third World'.[10] This means, therefore, that a significant part of the wealth of the industrialised nations has been generated through this imbalance in trade.

This phenomenon does not affect merely the acquisition of wealth. In the world we live in, *greater wealth means greater power*. Just when the former colonial countries were gaining their independence, they realised that their economic dependence was growing along with the other problems already mentioned. This state of affairs was defined by Kwame Nkrumah, former President of Ghana, as 'neo-colonialism'[11]: 'Neo-colonial policies are basically aimed at preventing newly independent countries from consolidating their political independence, so as to keep them economically dependent on the power of the world capitalist system. In the case of pure neo-colonialism, the assignment of economic resources, the thrust of investment, legal and ideological structures, together with other traces of the old society continue without change—except for the substitution of "internal colonialism" for "formal colonialism", i.e. the transfer of power by the former colonial masters to local ruling classes. In this situation, *independence has to be won in conditions that do not meet the basic needs of society*, and represents a partial denial of true sovereignty and a partial continuation of disunity within society. The most important branch of the theory of neo-colonialism is, therefore, the theory of economic imperialism'.[12]

The injustice of the present system of international trade means that, while on the one hand it *creates wealth and power for a minority* of the human race, on the other it *generates poverty and dependence for the great majority* of the countries of the world. History shows this process to be the result of a centuries-long evolution, within which the phenomenon of international domination, or *imperialism*, has made its presence felt and is still doing so.

4. A NEW TURN OF THE SCREW

Over the past fifteen years, the raw material-producing countries, that is those of the poor 'South', have tried *various means of breaking out of this situation of poverty and subjection*. For some time the international community saw *aid* as the best structure for overcoming these conditions. Just as the Marshall Plan had made a decisive contribution to the rebuilding of Western Europe, so plans of support were drawn up and offers of development aid made to the countries of Africa, Asia, Latin America, etc. What was not spotted, however, was that *there is no such thing as disinterested aid*. Theressa Hayter quotes President Kennedy as saying, in 1961: '... overseas aid is a method by virtue of which the United States maintains a position of influence and control throughout the world, and supports a good number of countries that would otherwise finally have gone under, or moved to the Communist bloc'.[13] Generally speaking, and especially in view of the financial terms imposed, one can say that the aid given by the rich countries to the underdeveloped ones is at least cancelled-out by the deterioration in the terms of trade.

This led some producers of raw materials, in the late sixties and early seventies, to organise *associations of producers* with a view to protecting the value of the products they put on the market. The best-known example of this attempt was the creation of OPEC (Organization of Petroleum Exporting Countries). The experience of such associations over the past fifteen years has shown that while they can raise prices in the market, this does not always mean that the resulting profits will be invested in the producing countries. Unfortunately, the security offered by investment opportunities in the wealthy nations is a stronger attraction than the possibilities for investing this new capital at home. So *old riches call to new riches. And the result is that the poor go on being poor*, without being able to fulfil their new hopes of a better life. (This is perhaps more true of the Latin American than the Gulf States members of OPEC with which English readers are more familiar.—*Trans.*)

But experiences like those of OPEC, or the aborted OCEC (Organization of Copper Exporting Countries, which never came into being thanks to the coup which overthrew Allende's government in Chile), also show that such associations can have considerable power. When OPEC was able to maintain its cohesion and increase the price of petroleum on the international market, the industrial nations were forced to make severe adjustments to their economies in order to cope with a situation in which they could no longer count on low cost energy sources.

This was the context in which President Nixon, in August 1971, decided to instruct the US Secretary of the Treasury to take the necessary steps to maintain the value of the currency. He asked Senator Conolly temporarily to suspend the convertibility of the dollar to gold. Since then there has been no fixed dollar-gold parity. In this way the United States found a way to go on printing dollars and paying its oil importing bill. This mass of hard currency went to the oil-producing countries, helping to swell the vast (unknown how vast) volume of petro-dollars. Inevitably, this introduced a great measure of instability into the financial markets of the world. The mass of petro-dollars was added to the mass of euro-dollars (built up thanks to the wages paid to American servicemen with NATO forces in Western Europe). One effect of this was to lower the exchange rate of the dollar, and therefore the cost of North American products, making them more competitive on the international market. But another, was to produce a surge of demand for dollars among the capitalists and governments of Third World countries. The dollar was cheap, but it was still a strong currency. So one had to have dollars. A little later, between 1973 and 1975, those who held the controlling interest in international finance (that is, those who administered these vast amounts of dollars) began to offer this 'cheap' money with the argument that debt was not necessarily an obstacle to development. It was then said that *'development consists in administering the debt'*. This was how many countries in the Third World contracted enormous debts which have mortgaged their futures for decades to come. 'The growth in the overall external debt of the underdeveloped countries was fastest in the early seventies. According to Morgan Guaranty Trust's *World Financial Markets*, the underdeveloped countries represented 9.3% of operations of longer-term Eurocredit in 1970, 30% annually between 1971 and 1974, and 51.2% annually between 1973 and 1977. Latest information puts the current level at 57.4% for the year 1979.'[14]

The dollar crisis provided a clear indication of the workings of the private international financial system. The underdeveloped countries play a key part in this process, for several reasons. First, because of the rate at which their loans from the system have increased; second, because of the relatively very high cost of servicing their external debt in relation to their volume of exports; and third, because these loans are concentrated in a few countries which have reached a certain stage of development but offer great possibilities for the future, such as Brazil, Mexico, the Philippines, Zaire, etc.

The burden of debt is a crushing one for most Third World countries. It is obvious that there can be no question of repaying this debt. The interest on it is barely being paid, and that only at the cost of enormous sacrifices by the people of the debtor nations. They have to export as much as possible in order to service the debt, which means putting their products on the market at the most competitive prices. This means paying the workers very low wages, thereby denying them the opportunity of a better life. Then, to avoid increasing the debt, they have to import as little as possible, thereby stunting their capacity for growth. At present, it is fair to say that most industrial and agricultural workers in countries such as Brazil, Argentina, Mexico, the Philippines, Zaire, etc., are working basically to *help the rich live better still*, in order to subsidise them. The 'development' of the poor countries has become a sheer struggle for survival.

Their situation became far more acute when, between 1980 and 1984, the *interest charged by the banks* on these loans was raised to an unprecedented level. Till 1978-9, the rate charged by the private banks of the North had varied between 6 and 8% per annum. Towards the end of 1979 it shot up to 20%, remaining at around 15% for several years. It began to come down in 1984, and now stands at around 9.5% (which is certainly higher than can be considered 'normal'). In Latin America alone (the most indebted region of the Third World), the interest due to the private international banks represented a sum of some 175 million dollars over no more than five years, according to Arne Clausen, the President of the World Bank.

This international usury is designed to consolidate the security of the rich. *But this security is bought with the blood of the poor.* The profit taken by the rich means premature death for those who in practice have no say and no chance in society. So we have the *basic contradictions of the system.* For example, in Mali, production reached very high levels, such as had never previously been achieved, while the population suffered hunger on an unprecedented scale. The workers work just to pay the debt, which feeds on the sacrifices of the poor. Just as first-born were once sacrificed to Moloch, so the lives of the poor are today sacrificed to Mammon. The interest on the debt is something that inescapably has to be paid, like a taboo that cannot be broken.[15]

The paradox reaches tragic proportions when one thinks that, in reality, it is not the rich who are 'owed'. The have seized the value produced by the poor. It is really the poor to whom repayment is due. Not only because justice requires it, but because they, through the unjustifiable sacrifice of themselves, of their very lives, have been nourishing the wealth of their oppressors.

Translated by Paul Burns

Notes

1. C. Furtado *Prefácio à Nova Economia Política* (Rio de Janeiro 1976) pp. 32-3. Furtado defines capitalism as 'a socio-political formation, that is a sort of power structure that imposes those social relationships in which profit is most easily turned into capital' (p. 37).
2. See E.J. Hobsbawn *Industry and Empire* (London 1968).
3. Furtado, the work cited in note 1, pp. 54-5.
4. The Brandt Commission *North-South: a Programme for Survival* (London & Sydney 1980) p. 36.
5. F. Froeble *et al. The internationalization of Capital and Labour* (Sternberg 1973) pp. 12-13.
6. R.H. Strahm *Pays industrialisés—Pays sous-développés* (Neuchâtel 1974) pp. 18-19.
7. S. Parmar 'Some Implications of Global Vision in the Setting of UNCTAD II' in *World Development: a Challenge to the Churches* ed. D. Munby (Washington & Cleveland 1969) p. 101.
8. *Ibid.* p. 101.
9. Strahm, the work cited in note 6, pp. 76-9.
10. P. Jalée *Le Pillage du Tiers Monde* (Paris 1965) p. 38.
11. K. Nkrumah *Neo-colonialism as the Last Stage of Imperialism* (Ghana 1965).

12. J. O'Connor 'The Meaning of Economic Imperialism' in *Readings in US Imperialism* ed. K.T. Fabb & D.C. Hodges (Boston 1971) p. 40.

13. T. Hayter *Aid as Imperialism* (Harmondsworth 1971) p. 5.

14. S. Lichtensztejn 'De la crisis del sistema financiero internacional. Condiciones generales e implicaciones sobre América Latina' in *Economía de América Latina* 5 (1980) p. 72.

15. J. Betting 'O Juro é Tabu' in *Folha de São Paulo* 19.12.85.

John Kavanaugh

The World of Wealth and the Gods of Wealth

Their idols are silver and gold,
The products of human hands
They have mouths but speak not;
They have eyes but see not;
They have ears but hear not ...
They have hands but touch not ...
Their makers shall be like them,
Everyone that puts their trust in them.

(Ps. 115)

The great paradox of finding one's identity in wealth is ultimately the paradox of all idolatries: entrusting ourselves to our products, our silver and golden gods, *we become fashioned—re-created—in their image and likeness.* Bereft of personhood and human sensibility, we lose our vision. We become voiceless, unable to utter words of life and love. We neither touch nor move. At best, we cling and watch and are watched, slavishly attached to the idol we worship. To make wealth one's god, is to become brittle and cold, to become like unto a thing, to become invulnerable, impenetrable, unliving.

It is true that material securities are not the only candidates for idol worship. One may hanker after spiritual self-righteousness, or worship ideology and party, or genuflect to the State, or substitute the powers of Church for empowerment by God. The worshipping of idols is not the exclusive preserve of the materially wealthy individual or the excessively indulgent nations of the North. Sin is not a function of class.

Yet, since one can most fully and authentically speak of one's own sin and grace, it will be the focus of this essay to criticise only the *idols of wealth as encountered by a person of the United States.* At the same time, I invite the

17

reader to apply the paradigm of idolatry to his or her own social and cultural context.

In my own country, a nation admittedly blessed in numerous ways, it must be confessed that 'products of human hands' have been enthroned as objects of devotion. Wealth has become a 'reality principle',—even a 'spirituality' principle—against which all of life is measured. American culture, with its artifacts, institutions, economic practices and media events, establishes a 'real world' which stands in profound opposition to the content and exercise of faith in Jesus Christ. It is a 'reality', moreover, which is dangerously close to depersonalising its own people by forming them in the image and likeness of the Wealth-god. Its people are evangelised by the media with a relentless, omnipresent intensity. At thirty-hours of television watching per person per week, passive attention to this medium is second only to work as the activity which dominates an American's life and consciousness.

The 'Good News of Wealth' is proclaimed in a 100 billion dollar-a-year advertising industry. It is legitimated by an epistemology whereby anything that is knowable must be merchandiseable. It is supported by a metaphysics wherein anything that is real must have a dollar value. It is expressed in an anthropology and ethic which justifies the expendability of human persons.

The Wealth-god, in its American form, is an idol which is trinitarian— showing the faces of consumerism, hedonism and nationalism. And its worshippers, reflecting those faces in their own lives, vow themselves to possessiveness, self-gratification and dominance.

1.   PERSONS AS POSSESSIONS: BECOMING LIKE THE IDOL.

... 'We Are All the Things You Are': Advertisement for Saks Fifth Avenue.

... 'I don't really love to shop, but I do love to buy . . . . Possession is the whole point. I like seeing the stuff around me like a security blanket': *Time*, 'The Shopping Addicts', 18 March 1985.

... 'You become a beautiful person if it turns out you're the richest man in America': W.F. Buckley, in a Round-Table discussion from *Harpers* Magazine, Jan. 1986.

... 'Sports is only the most visible manifestation of the voracity that now characterises all social relationships . . . Americans snort eighty-five metric tons of cocaine a year; they drop twenty tons of aspirin a day; they consume more drugs in greater variety than any other people on the face of the earth': Harry Edwards in *Harpers* Magazine, Sept. 1985.

... 'If greed is so unpopular, why did the voters overwhelmingly choose an administration that considers greed a national virtue? ... The most popular weekly TV shows are about the rich, the cruel and the greedy ... The most successful men in today's business world are those who have mastered the art of taking over a company, ripping it apart for their own profit and moving on to another unwary victim': Mike Royko, *Chicago Tribune*, 12 August 1985.

Idolising of wealth is an accepted and acceptable characteristic of American consciousness. The spirit of Capitalism equates buying with identity-formation. Recent polls reveal that making money has become the dominant motivation for students entering universities. Products are hailed as the new heroes. Cabbage Patch dolls are supplied with birth certificates; they marry, they go to summer camp.

For many of us, what is most real is the paycheck. Even for American religious communities, financial security looms large as the true providence. Retired persons perceive themselves as having little or no worth once they are removed from the cycle of productivity and payment. If as an advertisement for *Time* Magazine claims, 'we are what we eat, what we build, what we buy', then indeed, our very identities rest with the products of our hands. If Saks Fifth Avenue is 'all the things we are', then we are owned by that merchandiser, and we must buy ourselves back.

Since possessions ensure identity, the acquisition of them becomes a matter of life and death, a matter of our very essence. The more we have, the more we are. For Americans, as a national newspaper proclaimed, 'one is not enough': 63% of families own at least two automobiles, 50% at least two colour televisions, 33% at least two stereos, 13% at least two homes. 'Manic possessive' personalities, we are jokingly termed by a magazine catering to the affluent. Human growth is not measured in terms of nobility, depth, or wisdom; it is measured in terms of accumulation and aggrandisement.

People wholeheartedly dedicated to the possession of objects are inevitably diminished in their capacity and inclination for human intimacy and covenant. They are taught to seek out, as an advertisement for American Motors advised, 'a problem-free relationship' with the world of purchaseable commodities. The price of human love is too great, its covenants too demanding.

Possessions, lodged in the citadel of our selves, serve as deities providing us with significance and salvation. It should not be surprising, then, that powerful resistance is mounted against any authentic evangelisation of American culture. This is one of the reasons why the American bishops, in applying the Gospel to our economic life, have met with much hostility and resentment. It is claimed that faith must acquiesce to cultural imperatives and 'economic realities'. It is charged that the gospels are too time-bound, too utopian and too unrealistic for the contemporary world.

It could not be otherwise. For the invitations and demands of Christ are outright assaults upon commercial consciousness. They confound the unquestioned assumption that salvation and security are assured by amassing wealth. The only acceptable capitalist version of Christ is the reversed mirror image of its competing ideologies which transform Christ into a revolutionary or proletarian exclusivist. Americans, while raging at such distortions of the left, content themselves with a Jesus transformed into a white success story of privilege, power and affluence.

2. SEXUALITY, PLEASURE AND AFFECTION: IN THE IMAGE AND LIKENESS OF THE IDOL.

. . . 'Each month, more money is spent on one issue of *Penthouse* than has ever been spent on any magazine in the history of the world': *Advertising Age*, advertisement.

. . . 'There is no way I can sell the product without selling sex': Businessman quoted in *Time*, 23 Oct. 1985.

. . . 'Children take what they see in movies to be the adult world in operation—they tell you that . . . and the values in movies today are hedonism, sexuality, violence, greed, selfishness': Robert Coles, Harvard Child Psychiatrist in *U.S. News and World Report*, 28 Oct. 1985.

. . . 'Abandon yourself to pure decadence': Perfume Advertisement.

. . . 'How to Tell Your Men Apart in the Dark . . . The only thing they have in common is Yardley. And You': Advertisement for Cologne.

. . . 'In the average year, American TV viewers are exposed to 9230 scenes of suggested sexual intercourse, sexual comment or innuendo . . . On soap operas, fully 94 per cent of the sex involves people not married to each other': *T.V. Guide*, Nov. 23, 1985.

. . . 'SEX SELLS': Cover Story of *Saturday Review*, August, 1985.

In the United States, there has been a massive shift in the cultural consciousness of human sexuality over the past thirty years. Herbert Marcuse would have called it 'repressive desublimation', a phenomenon wherein the passion for truth and justice is chanelled into immediate gratification. We are taught to want it all and to want it now; and we are taught that wealth will give it to us.

The human body, no longer understood as the revelation of personhood in space and time, *has been reduced to a function of wealth*, a commodity for exchange and use, a way to make money. Human sexuality has become so morally neutral in the United States, that some of the most significant dimensions of personal intimacy, self-revelation and integrity are rendered inconsequential.

In every sense of the word, our bodies are merchandised. They are advertisements, billboards for products that provide legitimacy in the wearing of them. Rock Stars use crucifixes as erotica. The depersonalisation of women is pandemic in liquor advertisements, heavy metal music, endless videos. And in the absence of committed witness and critical analysis for the area of sexual integrity, the prevailing dogmas concerning american sex are propagated by slick magazines, Phil Donahue talk-shows and soap operas.

Only the highest ingenuousness can prevent us from seeing that Capitalism and its money-idol have become predominating influences on sexual understanding and behaviour in the United States. 'Money' itself, a weekly business magazine claimed, has become 'the New Sex'. Surely it is improbable that the phenomena of auto-eroticism, homo-eroticism, mechano-eroticism and fetishism are not in countless ways reinforced and legitimated by consumerism and commerce. It is naive to suppose that the fragmentation of relationships, the splintering of community and family, and the erosion of our capacities for intimacy are unrelated to the cultural imperatives of capitalism and its undivided devotion to wealth.

The marketing principles of television programmes, the financial attractiveness of spicy novels written by priests, the demand for outrageousness in the business of rock music, and the 'acceptability' which money bestows upon the most degrading forms of depersonalised sexuality are the stuff of mercantile eros where the practice of chastity appears quaint and permanent faithful commitment in marriage seems scarcely imaginable.

Consequently, in this privileged arena of human affectivity, where men and women might most consistently embody their identity and purpose, the mirroring of ourselves in the Wealth-idol has devastating effect. Recreated in the image and likeness of the things we worship, not only are we disenfranchised of our personhood, we are dispossessed of feeling and sexuality. Our very bodies are reduced to little more than commodities which hide, rather than reveal the truth of our personhood.

3.   DOMINATION: MASTERING THE IDOL TO BE MASTERED BY IT.

. . . 'Day and Night, America's youth are enticed by electronic visions of a world so violent, sensual and narcotic that childhood itself appears to be under siege . . . Television violence is so pervasive that the average high-school student by graduation day has seen 18,000 murders in 22,000 hours of

television viewing—that's twice as many hours as are spent in the class room':
U.S.News and World Report, 28 Oct. 1985.

. . . 'The suicide rate among young people has tripled in 30 years to reach
"epidemic proportions" . . . Half a million children try to kill themselves each
year': *Saint Louis Post Dispatch*, 11 Sept. 1985.

. . . '"Rambo: A quick $53 million in Blood Money" . . . "The character of
Rambo is a great identity character for young American Males", said the vice-
president of American Multi-Cinema. "It's got the violence, the revenge, the
one guy against the world appeal", says CinemaScore President Edward
Mintz. "I see it as a healthy antidote to . . . all the peace-love junk of the 60's"
says Art Murphy, an industry analyst for *Variety*': *USA Today*, 4 June 1985.

. . . The *New York Times*, July 14, noted that the U.S. Congress heard the
invocation of Rambo at least a dozen times in the discussion of aid to
Afghanistan. President Ronald Reagan quipped: having seen Rambo, he
knows what to do the next time his citizens are taken as hostages.

. . . On 27 June 1985, Jeffrey Hart, a conservative Catholic, in his syndicated column suggested that president Reagan make a speech ending with these
words: 'In the future, and on principle, we guarantee that we will retaliate for
the death or injury of any U.S. citizen at the rate of 500 to 1. As I speak to you,
I have received word that 15 Shiite Villages and their inhabitants no longer
exist.'

A culture that lusts for things, must necessarily lust for power. To lose the
security of wealth and possession would be to lose everything, even being
itself. Thus, things must be defended at all costs. The divinisation of property
requires the exaltation of power. It demands deliverance into its hands. The
bomb is rock and salvation.

The dream of domination through invulnerable self-defence and the
security of brute force is the stuff of inflated media paragons. Blandishments
of violence win elections and steadfast followers. The hunger for dominion
spurs our most childish fantasies of revenge, wherein we devastate and
eliminate the enemy so definitively that there is no possibility of retaliation.

The logic of domination replicates in a series of dialectical mirrors which
reveal us as a fierce nation that might topple governments at will—but only
for a 'good and noble reason'. We imagine ourselves as Rocky and Rambo
and Clint Eastwood dedicated to wiping out evil in the world—evil which is
always externalised into some other class, some other nation, some other
revolution or ideology.

The language of domination is 'Might makes right', and 'We can only
negotiate through strength'. It is spoken not only in national and political
discourse, however; it is huckstered endlessly in advertising: 'Two things you

always wanted: Money and Power', 'Satisfy your Lust for Power'. And it is also uttered in homes and communities where people display themselves before the living God as 'self-made men and women', who 'call their own shots', and who have 'pulled themselves up by their own bootstraps'.

And so the imperialism of the nation reverberates in the arrogance of self, with the method for establishing dominance in both cases being violence. Christ, with his methodology of love and non-violent confrontation is encountered as someone alien to nationalised faith. The cult of power rebukes adoration of the true God. It demands total loyalty, a wholeheartedness, an utter submission. It can tolerate no serious competitor.

Dominance, as with Property and Pleasure, exacts from its adherents the *cost of faith*. The only Christ that can be tolerated is a domesticated one, pressed into the service of nationalism, greed, and self-indulgence. And so, preachers of television, pastors in isolated and secure parishes, leaders of a nation will invoke the name of a saviour who cannot be found in the Gospels.

Worship of wealth ensnares its followers with a dread of losing what has become most real and dear, so real and so dear that it seems one might lose one's very life to let go. Such is the nature of all idols. We must kill or be killed in the face of any threat that our idol might be taken away or shattered. All persons, including ourselves, are expendable in the grip of its demands. It is bondage to such a heartless god that calls out for liberation.

Worship of wealth inverts the revelation of Jesus. In Him we find that everything of this earth, all the blessings of productivity and achievement, all human artifacts and technology are for persons. More wonderfully yet, we find that even our very God is *for* human persons. This is a revelation that assails any idolatry which sells salvation at the cost of human freedom and integrity.

It was, after all, in the name of another god-idol, a cherished security, that Christ himself was handed over to the powers of darkness.

'The chief priests and the pharisees called a meeting of the Sanhedrin. "What are we to do", they said, "with this man performing all sorts of signs? If we let him go on like this, the whole world will believe in him. Then the Romans will come in and sweep away our sanctuary and our nation." One of their number named Caiaphas, who was high priest that year, addressed them at this point; "You have no understanding whatever! Can you not see that it is better for you to have one man die for the people than to have the whole nation destroyed?"' (John: 11:47 ff)

The disaster and the tragedy was, however, this. The person they killed for the sake of their security, was their God.

Part II

'Blessed are you poor'—Election and Mission of the Poor

Juan Alfaro

God Protects and Liberates the Poor— O.T.

THE CREATION of Israel through the Exodus from Egypt, the Sinai Covenant and the establishment in the Promised Land, is filled with deep moral implications for today's world. The biblical narrations of the 'events' more than historical narrations, are pedagogical and theological presentations of the dynamic of divine liberation. Hermeneutics is always a decisive factor in the way these narrations are read.

1. THE HERMENEUTICS OF LIBERATION

The texts of Exodus as well as the Magnificat have become trodden ground during the last few years and little seems to grow out of new studies.[1] Some Latin American biblical writers associated with liberation theology speak of the paradigmatic value of Exodus as a parable of oppression. They, even if they warn against it, often take a simplistic and fundamentalistic approach to the text and its applications for their present situation. Others stress the ideal principles of liberation theology hermeneutics, pointing out in general terms that their situation is a privileged locus for interpretation of those biblical texts;[2] they also stress that all history, the Bible included, must be read from the perspective of the poor, their experiences and aspirations, and for the benefit of the poor; the praxis and actual involvement of the interpreter is a decisive factor in the interpretation,[3] for since the rich will find it difficult to enter the Kingdom of Heaven, they will also find considerable difficulty in understanding the Book of the Kingdom.

Latin American exegesis in the line of liberation theology has not made much progress in the last ten years, in part because these ideal principles of

27

exegesis are difficult to implement in real life and *a new path for exegesis has still to be opened*. We shall attempt to make a start in these pages. What some have called the hermeneutics of liberation or the 'option for the oppressed' hermeneutics does little justice to the ideal of key Latin American liberation theologians. Such hermeneutics are based on a consciously chosen pre-supposition for interpretation which will articulate one's commitment and goal.[4] It must be stressed that a subjective bias in favour of the poor can be as detrimental as a bias for the rich and the status quo. Both are scientifically indefensible even if one might be more understandable than the other.

The Bible was written in the Third World. By Third World we do not mean the political reality born in 1955 at the Bandung Conference, but the *socio-political situation of dependent and independent nations*, oppressed and oppressors, which has existed since the dawn of history. Israel was a Third World country, while Egypt, Assyria, Babylon, Persia and others took their turn as First World powers. The political, social, economic and even religious life of Israel was often at the mercy of these nations. The external dependence and oppression, as well as the condition of international politics, often resulted in internal divisions, tensions and oppression, as the prophetic texts eloquently proclaim. The Bible was written by persons in that concrete area of the world. Biblical authors had generally in common an ardent faith in the salvific power of Yahweh, a deep sense of social justice and a desire to motivate and challenge the readers and promote a change for greater justice. With this in mind, we might consider present parallel Third World communities committed to justice and motivated by faith as a privileged locus for understanding the Bible. They will need the help and criticism of scientific exegesis, but scientific exegesis cannot ignore their privilege.[5]

2.   SIGNIFICANCE AND CENTRALITY OF EXODUS

The theological significance of Exodus has been well stated by many writers. They see in Exodus the creation of a people out of the nothingness of slavery. It was not just a simple change of social conditions which would have made oppressors and oppressed trade places, but the *creation of a new social order called to eliminate all oppression*. It was an Exodus FROM a condition of slavery FOR a new life in brotherhood and justice.

The liberation process of Exodus started because God listens to the cry of the oppressed. That cry was more than a self-pitying complaint; it was an appeal to the justice of God in the face of human injustice. The God of life could not remain neutral in a situation of death; He had to commit Himself.[6] Only the wicked do not listen to the cries of the poor (see Prov. 21:13). God took side with the poor in such a way that the renewed efforts of the oppressor became sterile and the people continued to grow and multiply (see, for example, Exod. 1:9,12,20). Since in the Exodus God made an option for the poor, all misery and oppression is provisional, and liberation is promised on the horizon.[7] The oppressive Pharao 'who did not know Joseph' and 'was afraid' (see Exod. 1:8-10) of the oppressed, like every oppressor, would try to make the oppressed in his image and likeness, keeping them ignorant and fearful, but his efforts were doomed to fail. Pharao had a chance and a call to be a saviour and liberator of the slaves, but he hardened his heart and refused to listen to God. The oppressed on their part, once free, will have the temptation to become image and likeness of their oppressor, unless a dramatic change of heart takes place in them. That change was to take place through the Covenant of Sinai, the heart and centre of the Exodus.[8]

The liberation of the Exodus was to have a double dimension. The *external liberation* from racial, political, economic and religious oppression was to be consecrated and confirmed through the Covenant which offered the *internal liberation* from the shackles of the heart. In certain periods of the Old Testament history, the challenge of the Covenant was ignored and the Israelites reproduced in their land the conditions of Egypt (see 1 Kings 12:1-19); the prophets took care that the challenge was repeatedly heard. It was precisely in those periods when the story of the Exodus came to be written and was repeated, for it contained a call and a challenge to follow the divine plan of liberation and dignity for all. In the New Testament, Jesus opens his ministry with a call to an internal conversion which must produce fruits in new external social, political, economic and religious conditions of justice. Like the Jews of old, sometimes Christians seem to forget the full challenge of the (New) Covenant message.

The Exodus is often looked upon as a long march and a process of organisation of a people. The disorganised slaves of the beginning appear at the end as an army or a liturgical procession solemnly marching out from Egypt (see Exod. 12:37-42). On the other hand, as the Israelites get organised, their oppressors are gradually disorganised and divided, sealing their own doom (see Exod. 10:7). The Israelites, at the beginning, were so overwhelmed by the economic and political situation that they could not listen to or understand the message of liberation and the commitment of God to the poor (see Exod. 6:2-9).[9] At Sinai they were challenged to realise that they had been called from *servitude to service*.

3. LIBERATION AND CONFRONTATION: THE PLAGUES (EX. 7:1-12:42)

The account of the plagues, like other sections of the Book of Exodus, betrays a variety of literary strata, accumulation of traditions or documents, with subsequent incoherences, all woven together under an epic mantle into an artistic pedagogical unit. I cannot accept M. Noth's view that the story of the plagues has no real purpose and, hence, it must be directed exclusively towards the account of the Passover night without which it makes no sense.[10] As we shall see, it is precisely from our experience with present day faith communities and groups undergoing a struggle for their liberation that we can make sense and see the theological and pedagogical dimension of the narration as it stands. There is, also, in some authors, a fundamentalist tendency to see in the plagues echoes of a historical memory of natural calamities which periodically afflicted Egypt. It is my personal opinion that most of the plagues could better be of Palestinian origin but have been transplanted to an Egyptian setting. We must also refuse to see the God of the plagues as a 'miracle manufacturer', an image so pleasant for many Christians.[11]

Numerous authors have pointed out the artificiality of the account of the ten plagues. In Psalms 105 and 78 we find seven plagues, while the Yahwist and the Priestly traditions seem to have five. Since the narration of the tenth plague is so different from the preceding, it has been suggested that the tenth plague, originally, might have been the despoiling of the Egyptians which is so important as to be narrated three times (see Exod. 3:21-22; 11:2-3; 12:35-36). The darkening of the sun (ninth plague) has also been seen as parallel with the first plague, against the river, so that the two main gods and sources of life for Egypt are utterly defeated. In the present state of the text there is a correspondence between the first plague, when there was blood all over Egypt, and the last one in which the blood of the firstborn covers the land.

As the narration stands, and in the light of the experience of oppressed groups in the process of liberation, *a new understanding of the plagues becomes necessary*. The narration presents a well thought out description of the dimensions involved in a confrontation that leads to liberation.

Three of the plagues, in strategic places, are decisive in determining the aspects of the confrontation: *the third, the seventh and the tenth*. The introduction of the plagues in Exod. 7:1-2 gives a clue to the possible meaning of what follows. The narration opens with a *theological confrontation*. Moses is presented as a God, with Aaron as his prophet; they will confront Pharao, a god for the Egyptians, with his prophets the magicians. After the third plague the defeated magicians recognise on what side the true God really is (Exod. 8:15).

The fourth plague opens a new dimension of *political confrontation*. Moses is conceived as a political leader who confronts Pharao as a political leader and king of Egypt. As good politicians, they negotiate and Pharao offers a compromise: they can offer sacrifices 'in the land'. Moses asks for a three day journey into the desert and Pharao grants that they might be allowed to go provided they do not go too far (Exod. 8:21-24). This dimension of political negotiation is continued in the next stage after the eighth plague. The political dimension closes with the seventh and longest plague, the hailstorm in which the hand of God is recognised in the thunder, hail and lightning. Pharao, totally defeated, confesses his sin and offers permission to leave the land (Exod. 9:27-28).

After the seventh plague the narration offers a new dimension of *socio-economic confrontation*. Pharao confesses that he 'and his people' have been unfair (Exod. 9:27). Now not only the heart of Pharao, but also 'that of his servants' is said to be hardened (9:34; 10:1). The servants intervene after the eighth plague asking Pharao to let Israel go since the economic price they are paying is awfully high (Exod. 10:7). It is at this level of economic interests that death threats are heard (Exod. 10:27-29). The climax of the socio-economic confrontation comes when every Israelite is ordered to borrow objects of gold and silver from every Egyptian so as to leave them penniless. The rich are left empty while the poor go away enriched. The economic injustices of the past are in that way redressed. This economic punishment, planned by God, has to be executed by the 'clever' Israelites.

Levels of Confrontation:

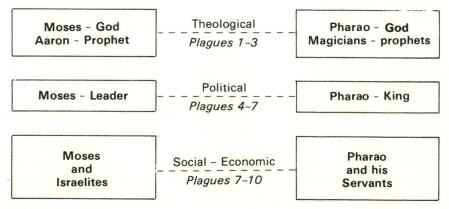

Moses - God Aaron - Prophet	Theological *Plagues 1-3*	Pharao - **God** Magicians - prophets
Moses - Leader	Political *Plagues 4-7*	Pharao - King
Moses and Israelites	Social – Economic *Plagues 7-10*	Pharao and his Servants

These three dimensions, theological, political and socio-economic, in concrete struggles for liberation, *do not come as successive stages*, but are integral dimensions of the whole confrontation for liberation. In every aspect of the struggle theological, political and economic realities are at stake. We know from experience that these dimensions are found in the struggles of oppressed groups. Thus, in the United States, when Caesar Chavez started his fight for basic human rights for farm workers in California, an important aspect of the fight was the support and blessing of organised religion declaring that justice, 'the finger of God', was on Chavez' side. The 'political' negotiations that followed failed because of bad will and lack of interest on the part of the agricultural growers. A socio-economic dimension became a necessity with a call for a general strike and the support of the public through the boycott of certain agricultural products; economic interests were at stake and violence and death followed before 'victory' was achieved.[12]

The same as in Exodus, when dealing with the cause of the poor, it is often next to impossible to separate racial and socio-economic aspects from the political and theological ones; this is specially true when the poor struggle also to be faithful to the biblical principles of peace, justice and love.

4. LIBERATION THROUGH THE COVENANT AND THE LAND

The Covenant of Sinai was to give its real meaning and depth to the liberation from Egypt. It aimed at the conversion of the heart of the people and looked forward to the future life in the Promised Land. The *land was to be a 'sacrament' of the liberation received* and the place where the ideals of the Covenant would become a theological, political and socio-economic reality.[13]

The Book of Exodus inserts the Code of the Covenant in the context of the Sinai Covenant and the Ten Commandments (see Exod. 20:22-23:33). Although the Laws of the Code derive from various historical periods, there is a common denominator in them, a strong concern for justice and the protection of the poor and the helpless.[14] Whenever oppression takes place, God will systematically take sides with the oppressed even if they are foreigners and not Jews (see Exod. 22:22,26; and see Deut. 24:10-22).

Poverty was to be either accidental or temporary for the individual person, although it would be an ever present social reality. The experience of Egypt was such that it was never to be inflicted on anyone. Even enemies were to be loved and foreigners were to be treated as neighbours and brothers (see Exod. 22:20; 23:9; Lev. 19:33-34). The proof of one's freedom of heart, then, even in the Old Testament, was to be shown by conquering evil through kindness (Exod. 23:4-5; Lev. 19:15-18).

The religious laws of the Code of the Covenant have a strong social and liberating dimension especially welcomed by the poor. The *Sabbatical rest* is important not so much because God rested on the seventh day but because on that day servants and foreigners can have their rest (see Exod. 23:12). The Sabbatical Year was most important for the poor because debts were to be cancelled and the fruits of the land were reserved for the poor (see Exod. 23:10-11). The Jubilee Year was to implement a general land reform programme that would give everyone, especially the poor, a fresh chance to open his or her way through life.

The land, a gift of the Lord for all the people, was to be the 'sacrament' that made real the liberty, dignity and security procured through the Exodus. In an agricultural economy, the possession of land was so basic that, to take away people's land was tantamount to condemning them or their family to poverty or slavery, frustrating the goal of Exodus. For this reason, the crime of landgrabbing, and even land accumulation, deserved the most exemplary punishments and curses.[15]

The goal of Exodus was the perfect brotherhood and freedom among Israelites which through the gift of the land would result in the elimination of all oppression, injustice and poverty. There was to be only one Lord, master and owner of all, God. The goal was to become a reality especially on the Year of the Lord, as outlined for the Sabbatical Year in Deut. 15:1-11; the biblical text presents the *ideal goal*, the *eventualities of life* and the *stark reality*:

15:4—The ideal: 'There will be no poor among you.'

15:7—The possibility: 'If there is among you a poor man, one of your brethren . . . .'

15:11—The Reality: 'For the poor will never cease out of the land.'

The Israelites would always find a challenge to charity and generosity through a duty towards the poor. Jesus quoted Deut. 15:11 to imply that if one truly cares for the poor one will always discover opportunities to help them (see Matt. 26:11). The words of Jesus, as well as those of Deut. 15:11, are often quoted to imply that, no matter what is done to eliminate poverty, all efforts are doomed to failure, hence, nothing should be done and resignation is the answer. Nothing could be farther from the biblical message, since the context of that text is one of the ideal towards which there will always be work to do. In a parallel manner, Jesus asked His disciples to 'be perfect just as the heavenly Father is perfect' (see Matt. 4:48). The point of the injunction is not its possibility or impossibility but the eternal quest for perfection as a goal of life.

The biblical history of Israel presents the *official model of what God does* *and wants to be done in every nation.* God wants everyone to have 'land', that is liberty, dignity and security. As societies move away in the course of the history from agricultural economies to industrialised and post-industrial settings, it will always be the task of Christians to strive so that no one be excluded from the blessings signified by a parcel of land. A well remunerated job, in some circumstances and with certain guarantees, could produce the same benefits in an industrial situation; 'going back to the land' and land reform are no longer a solution for many nations, but as humanity makes progress, there will always be the challenge to find ways and forms of providing everyone with the basic rights given through Exodus and the Land.

Great sectors of humanity do not enjoy today the basic blessings intended by God for all. Many nations are still struggling today for political, social and economic rights; some have no liberty, security and even dignity nor a real chance of making it in our world. God does not want that. Their struggles for liberation are theological. The life of nations and not of individuals is in the hands of a few. They can listen to the cries of the poor and of the victims of perpetrated poverty, *'los empobrecidos',* as they are being called in Latin America, since they have a big say on their fortunes. Like the Pharao of Exodus, they are challenged to be liberators but they can also chose to continue being oppressors. As in biblical times, the poor remain a reality challenging our fairness and generosity. God and the future are on the side of the poor. God made an option for the poor and invites us to do the same. We have to be on God's side, the winning side.

Notes

1. A good bibliography on the subject is found in F.A. Pastor 'Liberación y Teologia' *Est. Ecle.* 56 (1981) 355-356.

2. See L. Boff *El Rostro Materno de Dios* (Madrid 1979) pp. 221-222.

3. See G. Gutierrez *La Fuerza Historica de los Pobres* (Salamanca 1982) pp. 13-14.

4. See E.S. Fiorenza *In memory of Her* (New York 1983) p. 6; 'Tablesharing and the Celebration of the Eucharist' in *Concilium* 152 (2/1982) pp. 3-12.

5. An excellent book on this topic is that of C. Mesters *Flor Sin Defensa* (Bogota 1984).

6. See J. Plastaras *The God of Exodus* (Milwaukee 1966). See also, W. Brueggemann 'A Shape of Old Testament Theology, II: Embrace of Pain' CBQ 47 (1985) 401-402; E. Gesternberger 'Jeremiah's Complaints' JBL 82 (1963) 397-408.

7. See G. Gutierrez *A Theology of Liberation* (Maryknoll 1973) pp. 154-160.

8. This theme is well developed by P. Freire in *Pedagogy of the Oppressed* (New York 1982); also by J.S. Croatto in *Exodus. A Hermenutics of Freedom* (Maryknoll 1981).

9. See J.L. Sicre *Con los Pobres de la Tierra. La Justicia Social en los Profetas de Israel* (Madrid 1984) p. 52.

10. See M. Noth *Exodus* (Philadelphia 1962) pp. 68-69.

11. See J.L. Cunchillos *La Biblia. Una Lectura Catequética del Antiguo Testamento—I* (Madrid 1974) p. 113.

12. A struggle along the same lines, though without violence or death, took place in San Antonio, Texas, where Mexican Americans through the Communities Organized for Public Service (COPS) struggled to redress secular injustice and discrimination so as to enjoy full civil, political and economic rights. The churches took sides with the poor, proclaiming their cause as a theological issue; after long negotiations and economic pressures 'victory' was achieved.

13. See J. Alfaro 'The Land—Stewardship' *BTB* 8 (1978) 51-61; see also, W. Brueggemann *The Land: Place as Gift, Promise and Challenge in the Biblical Faith* (Philadelphia 1977).

14. The same concern appears in the sections of the 'Code of Holiness' that have contacts with the Code of the Covenant: see Lev. 17-26, esp., 19:1-33 and 25:23-55.

15. See 1 Kings 21:1-29; also, in Deut. 27:17, the third curse against 'prevalent' sins in the period of the monarchy is directed against land robbers or displacers of landmarks.

Georges Casalis

For Human Beings, Impossible!

'He has shown strength with his arm,
he has scattered the proud in the imagination of their hearts,
he has put down the mighty from their thrones,
and exalted those of low degree;
he has filled the hungry with good things,
and the rich he has sent away empty.

(The Magnificat, Luke 1:51-52)

THE GOSPEL is a universal message of liberation but it is manifested in a divided world, and so it has a different impact on different people. Its feel and effect are different according to whether it is a matter of the poor or of the rich being liberated. To the former what is announced is a change for the better, the end of their centuries long oppression and humiliation, whereas to the latter it is the fact that from now on they are stripped of the wherewithal to humiliate and oppress and that the insurrection of the poor is bringing about the end of their privileges and exemptions *now*—in a process that will come to its term in the Kingdom. So in various ways, both opposed and convergent, some are freeing themselves and others are being freed, and wherever this is happening the outlines of a new civilisation are taking shape—a 'civilisation of love' as the fathers gathered at Puebla in 1979 put it. It is a civilisation in which it is possible to see the growth of the 'tree of peace the roots of which are justice in all domains', as the refrain of the meeting of the World Council of Churches held at Vancouver in 1983 has it. Human completion excludes oppression suffered as much as oppression perpetrated; it demands 'the replacement of the right of might by the might of right' (Girardi). Jesus' appeal, that is to say his exacting grace, as this emerges from the gospels, has a healthy radicality about it in this regard. And here we cannot evade the great prophetic challenge of Dietrich Bonhoeffer: 'Cheap grace is the deadly enemy of our Church. We are fighting today' (the text dates from 1937: he is talking about the spiritual *and* the political resistance to National Socialism, which for the author issued in martyrdom, on 8th April 1945) 'for costly grace . . . . Cheap grace means the justification of sin without the justification of the sinner. Grace alone does everything, they say, and so everything can remain as before. "All for sin could not atone." . . . Well, then, let the Christian live like the rest of the world . . . . Let him not attempt to erect a new religion of the letter by endeavouring to live a life of obedience to the commandments of Jesus Christ. The world has been justified by grace. The Christian knows that and takes it seriously . . . . Cheap grace is grace without discipleship, grace without the cross, grace without Jesus Christ, living and incarnate. Costly grace is the treasure hidden in the field; for the sake of it a man will gladly go and sell all that he has. It is the pearl of great price to buy which the merchant will sell all his goods . . . . It is the call of Jesus Christ at which the disciple leaves his nets and follows him . . . . Such grace is costly because it calls us to follow Jesus Christ. It is costly because it costs a man his life, and it is grace because it gives a man the only true life. It is costly because it condemns sin, and grace because it justifies the sinner. Above all it is costly because it cost God the life of his Son . . . . Costly grace is the Incarnation of God' (*The Cost of Discipleship*, London, S.C.M. 1959, pp. 35-37).

So the more God thwarts human beings, the more he is for them; the more Jesus condemns the rich, the more he hopes and desires the emergence of their true face, that of their birth (James 1:23), the more he wants them to take their place with everybody else in the midst of the fraternal and equal community that attests the recapitulative design of God in the world in process of becoming the Kingdom. Rather as the word of the prophets of the first Testament did, the messianic word says 'No' only in order to say the Father's 'Yes' more emphatically, this father who because he is the origin of all life, wants it to be free and happy for all his children without exception or distinction.

Jesus' love for the rich man (Mark 10:17-31): Matthew (19:16-30) and Luke (18:18-30) were afraid of the rigour of the original story preserved by Mark. Whereas the latter is careful not to be to precise and speaks of a rich man in general, the two others try to make an exception of him, a particular case: a 'young man' (Matthew) whose age should make one indulgent or a 'ruler' as it were 'quite naturally' seeking from Jesus, if not honours, at least the approval lavished on him everywhere else. Above all, however, the two 'great synoptics' strip the confrontation of the profoundly human character it has in Mark's account by omitting the double mention of the 'regard' or 'look' Jesus gives his interlocutor and especially the astonishing mention of the love that draws him to the man and which is no doubt the key to the whole of the original text. It is a text that is unique among Jesus' encounters.

It is in fact a man who is aging, speaking of his youth with a certain nostalgic distance, who comes up to Jesus and, with a rare gesture reported only two other times in the gospels in connection with 'seekers of miracles' and once to characterise the derision of the soldiers who torture the man condemned to death (see Matt. 17:14 and Mark 1:40 and 15:19) he throws himself at the feet of Jesus. This rather theatrical gesture shows the importance he attaches to the question he is going to put. And he does this at a moment when Jesus, having already twice announced his passion, sets out on a new phase of his journey to Jerusalem . . . . 'Good teacher': to be sure, it is the only time a text of the gospel reports Jesus having been addressed in this way and the only time too that Jesus senses 'the obsequiousness and flattery of the rich man's presenting himself as not just anybody but somebody rather different from these wretched rustics who make up his habitual following. By refusing his praise and by redirecting to God alone the goodness attributed to him in order to win his goodwill, Jesus is refusing every categorisation of humanity, every way of setting human beings apart, be it social, moral, religious or and above all (as will be said later in the infinite speculations of theological treatises) metaphysical! He wants to be an ordinary man, in no way different from other mortals: faced with the unique Good, creator and liberator of all human beings and their environment, animal, vegetative, and material, no discrimination, no ethnic or spiritual superiority holds water. Jesus himself knows this and wants to be a man like anybody else, completely identified with others, and it is only in this way that he can also be 'for others'. If this is not the case, then Bonhoeffer's Christological definition, 'Jesus Christ, the man for others' corresponds to no reality; it is no more liberating that the pseudo-human adventures of all the gods and goddesses of the various pantheons. It is just because he knows and perfectly respects the distance that separates him from the Father, it is just because he wants in no way to grasp the divine condition (Phil. 2:6), it is just because he remains completely identified with humanity to the point of dying as a result that the first profession of his divinity is born on the lips of a non-disciple, a Roman centurion to boot: 'Truly this man was the Son of God' (Mark 15:39) . . . . It is his poverty, his destitution, his impotence, and not some aristocratic pre-eminence, or thaumaturgic power, that transforms the human condition, opening the door to reconciliation by means of the solidarity he practises and communicates. Once again it is the Bonhoeffer of *Letters and Papers from Prison* who gathers up the entire heritage of Eastern spirituality and Lutheran theology so deeply marked by it and thereby provides the Christological basis to the challenge and promise represented by the poor in the face of all the sufficiencies and bastilles of the rich.

The rich man put the question what he should *do* to inherit eternal life and Jesus for his part took seriously that *practice* that in the flux of history, in the 'penultimate' phase of existence attests and looks forward to the fullness of life. So, quite naturally, like any other pious Jew, he refers back to the Torah: isn't it 'the law of liberty' (James 1:25), the very form taken in the life of the people of God by the Covenant by which the God of Life puts himself at the service of the whole of humanity? So, if the rich man is really serious about the question of true life, he should assess himself and draw up a balance sheet of his relationships with his neighbour. Curiously enough what is in question here is only the commandments of the second table, cited without order and incompletely—the point being that the service of God is in good shape when that of others is assured. Doing the will of God in the community and society, getting one's *orthopraxis* right is the first condition of a right confession of faith, it is being in *orthodoxy*.

With a really breath-taking aplomb the rich man responds by saying, apparently without a moment's hesitation, 'Teacher, all these I have observed from my youth.' What comes to expression here is the perfectly good conscience, the sentiment of the Pharisaism of observance, the very definition of a religion the exemplary seriousness of the forms of which dispenses its adherents from penetrating where everything is decided, the heart of the matter, which is also the human heart. How can one be sure that it is not divided, that it burns with a pure love at every moment and that if the Law is given for the sake of life it does not become the legitimate spring-board for self-aggrandisement by which a person who wants to 'thank God that he is not like the rest of men, extortioners, unjust, adulterers . . . ' puffs himself up like somebody mounting his high horse? That frightful religious pride, shot through with disdain for all those who are not disciples, that judgment on all those who do not identify with the behaviour of a group considered to be exemplary and the carriers of the world's health, all this is exposed to the light of day in the presence of the one whose combat will bring him to the inevitable term of the united struggle of all the earth's damned: the cross, martyrdom, death in utter dereliction . . . .

This is just where there emerges, like a diamond from its gangue, the point of the story that Matthew and Luke were not able to preserve, the miracle of the Gospel: 'And Jesus looking upon him loved him.' There are many passages in the gospels in which it is a *look* of Jesus that is decisive, that is to say, a reading in depth of reality as a whole and of each of the people he engages with that penetrates all masks, discovering the person behind the persona, the truth of things behind ideological mirages. There can be no doubt but that according to the text the rich man finds himself in front of a mirror that reflects his own image without any fear or flattery. His situation is like that of king Belshazzar at his macabre feast: Jesus' look intimates to him his definitive Mene, Tekel and Parsin—the days of your power have been numbered and are slipping away, you have been weighed in the balance and found wanting, you are divided against yourself because your having has made you lose the sense of your being (see Daniel 5). A profound contradiction has taken hold of you: you want to *do* something in order to inherit eternal life, whereas *the doing characteristic of having* is sterile because it serves only to increase desire, passions and envies that are so many forms of idolatry. Only the *doing characteristic of being* expresses life because, rather than attesting the pride and lust for power of the predatory creature, it is the logical and consistent consequence of the irruption into somebody's life of the 'grace that is costing'. The self-aggrandisement that, according to the letter to the Romans, is the very essence of sin leads to the vanity and nonsense of having. Faith that is 'the hand of the souls receiving Jesus Christ offered by the Gospel' (Calvin) is walking behind Jesus, on the path of the disinterested service and solidarity that are the very forms of the new being.

We cannot take it for granted that Jesus loved this Pharisee. What we are faced with is the paradox of the Gospel indicated above: it is by strongly attacking the doing characteristic of having that Jesus hopes to provoke in him the flow of the ethic of being. It is, therefore, not by reason of any superficial sympathy or natural inclination that Jesus loves him but despite the fact that he is fundamentally antipathetic and fundamentally in error and/or *because that is how he is.* That is why he came, not for the well but for the sick, not for the 'just' (?) but for sinners. He loves the rich man in the way that God always loves, in the way that Hosea loved his unfaithful prostitute of a wife, in the way that God loves his very enemies: 'even when we were sinners through our trespasses, he made us alive together with Christ (by grace you have been saved), and raised us up with him, and made us sit with him in the heavenly places in Christ Jesus . . . it is the gift of God—not because of works, lest any man should boast. For we are his workmanship, created in Christ Jesus for good works, which God prepared beforehand, that we should walk in them' (Eph. 2:5-10). Doing is not a pre-condition but a consequence of the 'inheritance of eternal life'; it is not doing that liberates us but we are not liberated without doing!

This is just what motivates the insistence of Jesus who, behind the affluence of the rich man, descries lack, deficiency, emptiness and penury beyond measure. His wretchedness consists not so much in his having in itself as in his inability to give, to share, to get back to the economic and psychological level of the poor and, thereby, to become mobile enough to *follow Jesus* on his way to the cross: in order to rediscover the true sense of his life, to share in the heavenly treasure that is nothing but the universal and liberating paternity of the God of life, to be cured of the chronic misery that consists in his being isolated by his having. All that he needs to do is to listen to the mute appeal of the poor and to respond to it. They are, therefore, there as those who challenge him: Rejoin us, rejoin the Father; rid yourself of everything that separates you from us and you will enter into a living communion, a communion of freedom and hope with all the adopted children, who may have been enemies before but are now reconciled, disciples of Jesus and members of the body of Christ. But there is nothing more dangerous than the paths of freedom. Just as the journey into the desert occasioned the people to mutter against Moses and to regret the 'flesh-pots of Egypt', the invitation to engage in the exodus out of all socio-religious conformisms in order to enter into the transforming conformity with the man from Nazareth rouses not so much joy, gratitude and the relief of escaping from the gilded cage as depression, darkness of mood and a recoil as slow and silent as the first intuition had been swift and sudden as a thunderclap . . . .

This is where Jesus' second look fits in—a look no longer at the man who has already distanced himself from the Gospel but on all those who were involved in the incident which has just closed . . . .

'How hard it will be, how hard it is . . . ' twice, as if carried on a sigh from Jesus' heart, this utterance emerges to underline how radically closed the rich are to the appeal God makes to them in the poor. There is no 'doing' that leads to eternal life apart from the response to the precise indication given by Jesus; entry into the Kingdom cannot be bought or merited, it is opened up only by the violence of love, of life given, poverty shared. Only *death* to the will to have, to exercise power and to gain knowledge *for oneself*, in order to make oneself superior and to use instead of to serve, only the 'paschal passage' (Paulo Freire) can give the camel the thread-like quality that enables it to pass through the shaping eye of the needle. Only the memory of baptism and meditation on the mystery of the cross make the rich man rise again as somebody open and fraternal to others; only conversion to the poor forces open the closed door of all those who exploit others and yet at the same time want to 'scale heaven' (Luther). God gives himself gratuitously but he refuses himself to anyone who refuses to abandon himself to him.

Kierkegaard is always there to warn all readers of this story who would as a result tend to despise and condemn the rich man who turns his back on Jesus and abandons the road to Calvary to return to his comforts. Commenting on the parable of the tax-collector the Danish seer exclaims: 'There is another sort of hypocrisy or type of hypocrite that is like that of the Pharisee even though it takes the tax-collector as a model . . . they murmur hypocritically: "My God, I am thankful that I am not like this Pharisee . . . " . . . hypocrisy has picked up the trick of changing its mask, but it has remained substantially the same—or rather it has become worse . . . ' (*The Tax-Collector*). This, it seems, is what the disciples grasped: every interior self-distancing from the enemy and the denier of the Gospel immediately makes one like him or her. The rich man is only openly what I am shame-facedly; I conceal what he declares, what I should not hesitate to act out if I had the chance to do so. So the only thing to do is to fight against myself in fighting against him and to take advantage of the searing love of Jesus by manifesting to the rich man the resistance of the love of the Gospel, that astonishing tension between a refusal to collude and hope against hope . . . in what? in whom?—if not in a 'love stronger than death' (Song of Solomon 8:6). This is the meaning of the anxious question the disconcerted disciples put to him: 'Who then can be saved?' There is no answer to this except that God remains the ultimate possibility of liberation for all those who, whatever their possessions, remain accomplices in all forms of oppression and slaves of the gods of death. That is why we have to go on reading the two apparently contradictory beatitudes in their mutual confrontation: Luke's version in 6:20 that concerns exclusively the economically poor and Matthew's in 5:3: 'Forward, those who have been winded' (as Chouraqui would translate)—envisaging as the latter does all those who realise that it is *not enough to answer Jesus' appeal to be materially stripped in order to be free of all envy* and, moreover, to be really like, with and for others, in the same boat, sharing the same thirst for what will finally make the world a place we can all live in. 'But woe to you that are rich, for you have received your consolation' (Luke 6:24). This is the worst condemnation, addressed to those who take their stand on being included in a world banquet or a social class in which millions are spent every day to enable them to survive and to enjoy their culture and their security—with all the crazy and criminal production and sale of arms that this involves—and who, for forty eight hours see on television little Omayara, caught in the mud from the eruption of Nevado del Ruiz in agonies in Columbia for lack of a simple pump that would have allowed her to have her life saved. Perpetual representative of all the poor abandoned at the doors of us rich, she was and remains the personal and collective Lazarus of the 'Third World' dying of material technical and cultural destitution in the midst of our glutted opulence . . . . Of course the rich also know misfortune but it is when it strikes the poor that it takes on the character of a curse!

That following Jesus and responding to the appeal of the poor is neither sad nor frustrating is well brought out by Peter's question and the response he gets: breaking with the dominant family and social code, before the entry into the kingdom, access to a communion, a sharing, an equality the resulting joy of which declares in the very midst of the inevitable persecutions that it is under the sign of life and no longer of death that the disciples go forwards: 'We know that we have passed out of death into life because we love the brethren' (1 John 3:14). It is now that death has been conquered, which means that we can no longer lose our lives. As Uriel Molina, a priest in an heroic quarter of Managua, said to me in 1980 in the course of speaking of the two hundred and fifty 'muchachos' and 'muchachas' of his parish who had died in the war against Somoza: 'If they had not experienced the resurrection, they would not have died like this . . .'. This is the spirit in which Louis Aragon after the liberation of France wrote a hymn in memory of the Communist members of the underground under the title: 'Ballad of the Man who Sang through his Tortures' . . . . Wherever it comes from, withersoever it leads, solidarity is Life and Joy.

Signs and signals of the poor: Ruined by the numerous treatments of her ineffectual doctors, *the woman with the issue of blood* is not going to make a conspicuous entry onto the scene of the Gospel: in contrast to the rich Pharisee she comes to touch Jesus from behind, silently, 'like anybody else'. It is by making no special claim on him that one receives his grace (Mark 5:25-34). The widow who throws two small pieces into the temple treasury is *regarded* (!) by Jesus as having given all she had, all her life (Mark 12:41-44), 'out of her poverty' (out of her destitution, as it could also be translated). Like the widow of Sarepta (1 Kings 17) she shows that a rich person like the Pharisee is inevitably tied to *having*, out of which, if he is generous, he can give some *thing*, whereas when a poor person, in this case the widow herself, shows her solidarity it is herself, her life, her *being* that she offers. In this way, the poor person is like God who loves only in giving himself, that is to say, in risking himself to the limit, without reservation, protection or guarantee, losing his life in order to save and free that of all humankind and thereby realising the meaning of history . . . . Zachaeus is the antithesis of the rich Pharisee. It is quite true that he begins by raising himself above the common people, but the evangelist wittily makes the point that this man who is big in wealth is small in size (Luke 19:1-10) and that, in any case Jesus' invitation soon makes him come down *quickly* from his sycamore and disappear into the midst of the great mould of the crowd: a 'vertical' conversion, whereas the rich Pharisee refused to follow a path! Above all, however, he is going to cross the two thresholds to liberation into life: a poor man because he is in the social and religious margins of life, he is *regarded* and welcomed by Jesus who comes into his home; rich because he has great possessions, he discovers on meeting with Jesus that from now on life is to consist in sharing and in making good wrongs committed against another. Going beyond the requirements of the Jewish law he applies to himself the most rigorous sanction against thieves in Roman law, thereby confessing the iniquitous and guilt-laden character of his wealth (of all wealth?). And Jesus proclaims that the salvation of liberation has come to this man's family and business: there has been a reconciliation. His word has made a predatory sinner into a son of Abraham: somebody who from now on walks by faith and has received justification—the yes that God pronounces on the life of 'those who yield to him despite themselves' (Luther). This Zachaeus who tumbles down from the tree and manifests that the impossible possibility of God is happening is decisive—in the shape of the *conversion of the rich* refinding, or finding for the first time, the freedom to be a true being, in the likeness of God and his or her image . . . . In Vietnam, in 1973, some rich people came to testify to us that in stripping them of their possessions the Revolution had made true men and women out of them, no longer separated by anything from their people. This is the violence of popular uprisings, always provoked by 'institutionalised violence'. There is no question of sacralising it, but it nevertheless corresponds to the subversion of the established order inaugurated by the entry into history by the carpenter of Nazareth! When Paul the apostle relates how Christ stripped him of his entire Pharisaic inheritance to the point that he considered as so much 'dung' what had previously been the very basis of his religious and social conscience, he thinks of himself as being rapidly en route for the goal he hopes to attain, to 'seize' it because he has himself been 'seized' by Jesus Christ (Phil. 3:14). This is the end of an established existence, of security, the beginning and pursuit of a march in which, like Abraham, he continues without knowing where it will lead, from certainty to certainty, from beginning to beginning. And if he writes (2 Cor. 8:9): 'You know the grace of our Lord Jesus Christ, that though he was rich, yet for your sake he became poor, so that by his poverty you might become rich', what is clear is that the richness here attribted to Christ is that neither of having nor of power but that of grace alone, that of life given and abandoned in love. And the 'richness' communicated to Christians by the self-stripping of Christ consists precisely in that liberty that they are given to be able in their turn to enter into the dynamic of the liberating gift because it is made without calculation or reservation.

For the rest, the whole of the Gospel announces the reversal of social hierarchies and the rehabilitation of the poor. The text of Mark 10:17-31 concludes with an affirmation that must certainly not be limited to the spiritual realm alone: 'But many that are first will be last, and the last first. Some of the first are, therefore, left the possibility of remaining the first, that is to say, of coming down to the same level as everybody else, with the same rights and the same duties (Zachaeus, Saul of Tarsus, the publican and the Pharisee converted by the same encounter with liberating love!). But all the 'last' will be first, not because their poverty alone puts them 'naturally' on God's side but because God, incorrigibly, antecedently, has come out on their side, definitively. Hence the great invitation to rejoin them, while taking into account everything that resists the march towards and with them. And so that nobody may miss the point, we find in the foreground of the stories, alongside the *widows*, all the other rightless ones charged with the mission to prophesy: the *shepherds*, for the most part rustics and slaves, whose testimony is not admissible in court, are called upon to announce the Christmas event to the world (and that in texts as recent as those of the 'infancy gospels'!); *women*, a legally and ideologically negligible portion of patriarchal society, are chosen to be the first witnesses of the Easter happening about which they have to convince the incredulous apostles; *children*, who are not considered to have a personality until, in the case of boys, they are integrated by initiation into the society of adults, are taken by Jesus as the existential parables of the newly-born in the Spirit entirely dependent on the love of the Father and therefore able to live already in and for the kingdom; the *foreigners*, ranging from the magi from the East at the crib to the Roman centurion at the cross, and including the Syro-Phoenician woman and the centurions at Capharnaum and Caesarea and even the Gentiles of Romans 2:14, who are simultaneously of the number of those who take the Kingdom by force, getting in as it were by breaking in, and of those whose spiritual violence and moral rigour are held up as examples to pious Jews; the *tax-collectors and prostitutes* who, like many of the foreigners, are there to indicate that poverty may in the first place be material but that it has other faces, tied to the existence of social classes and religious castes—the very fact of the discrimination to which they are subject makes them particularly vulnerable to the call of Jesus, being all the more ready to walk after him for scarcely having any roots or homeland, which is why they are already way ahead of all those bogged down by rites and customs; and then finally *slaves* alienated by belonging to somebody else whose thing they have become and whose condition, according to Philippians 2:6 ff., Christ took on fully, washing the feet of his disciples and asking those who follow him not to think they are indispensable or even important: 'just slaves who only do what is their duty' (Luke 17:7-10). Most translations fudge the harshness of this word *doulos*, slave, but it is not only the one that Paul the apostle uses to describe himself as belonging to Christ but the one he uses at the end of Romans 6 to characterise the impossibility of neutrality in the human condition: one is either slave of sin unto death or else slave of justice unto life. This second slavery is in fact the 'glorious liberty of the children of God'.

We find in the second Testament at once the accents of an Amos lashing the rich who despise the poor and exploit their agricultural workers (James 2:1 ff. and 5:1 ff.), which amounts to the same thing, and the visionary utopia of Isaiah who announces the coming of a reconciled world, a society without cultural, religious, classist or sexist discrimination: 'For as many of you as were baptised into Christ have put on Christ. There is neither Jew nor Greek, there is neither slave nor free, there is neither male nor female' (Gal. 3:27-28). It is no doubt no accident that it is the most universal poverty, that of woman humiliated under every regime that is mentioned by way of a climax of the appeal and of the promise that reverberates through all the life and message of Jesus the liberator of the world . . . .

Because we have to stop . . . : 'Wir sind Bettler, das ist wahr' (we are beggars, that's the truth): these are the last words Luther wrote in the room in which he was destined to die, on 18th February, 1546. This was neither resignation nor false modesty but like the 'base line' of the two theses of the little book 'of the liberty of the Christian': 'The Christian is a free lord, he is subject to no-one. The Christian is in every respect a servant and he is subject to everybody.' Spiritual poverty, thirst for the Spirit and solidarity in love and the will to establish here and now the justice that is their 'flowering and triumphant coming' (Bernanos) . . . .

It is clear that whoever commits himself to the path that, logically, leads to the cross experiences the open and intimate rupture of conversion and so becomes a 'traitor' to his social and religious milieu and must expect to suffer all its consequences. This is the meaning of the terrifying words: 'If any one comes to me and does not hate his own father and mother and wife and children and brothers and sisters, yes, and even his own life, he cannot be my disciple' (Luke 14:25-27). Once again there can be no compromise between conforming and being transformed (see Rom. 12:1-2).

To conclude, we have been speaking from the beginning to the end of our brief reflection on the exacting love of Jesus but this means that it is not a matter of falling into a new legalism: the appeal is grace, the response to it liberty. Therefore the saying 'You cannot serve God and mammon' (Matt. 6:24) is a question not of the moral order but of the logic of grace: You cannot do it *any longer*, you have escaped from the clutches of money, you have been freed to serve God, that is to say, freed to respond to the plea of the poor and to share in their struggles for the transformation of the world and their hope for 'a new heaven and a new earth where justice reigns'.

Translated by John Maxwell

Notes by way of postscript

1. In a jointly-authored book that, to my knowledge, exists only in the German edition (*Die Bibel als politisches Buch*, Berlin/ Kolhammer T-Reihe 655 pp. 47-56), I have tried to relate Jesus' social option to the theological reading of it that the apostolic generation made. In a nutshell: it is by identifying himself with the wretched and by shouldering all the consequences of this choice and maintaining this faithfully to the point of dying for it that he becomes the creator of new life for the masses.

2. I could within the limits of this article only sketch the ecclesiological dimension of the question but it has been amply elaborated in the memorandum submitted by the Fédération Protestante de France *Église et pouvoirs*, of which I happened to be one of the authors and which was published in 1972. We concluded that a critique of the possessions, expertise and power of the churches—what they have, know and can do— was capital for the re-birth of a true prophetic ministry among them. The text has been translated into many languages and can be obtained from the Fédération Protestante de France, 47 rue de Clichy, 75009 Paris.

3. Apart from the major texts of the basic communities of Latin America and the writings of the liberation theologians the world over, it is always worth re-reading Bernanos' *Journal d'un curé de campagne*, in which the dialectic between social and spiritual poverty is represented with an admirable prophetic violence in the words of Dr Dalbende . . . who states that he is incredulous . . . .

Part III

The Poor in the Christian Tradition

Rainer Kampling

'Have We Not Then Made a Heaven of Earth?' Rich and Poor in the Early Church

INTRODUCTION

WEALTH AND poverty are concepts that need to be seen in their *social context* for their precise meaning to become clear. The poor man or woman of the *Roman empire* is characterised by lack of food, education, freedom, often also health and power. The poor included both those who had to toil for their living and also those who were dependent on the contributions of others. Their social status was zero. The rich person on the other hand had possessions and thus power. He had the opportunity to assert himself and his interests over against the State and the society whose respect he enjoyed. There were of course certain gradations, for example between the prosperous merchant and the possessor of enormous estates or latifundia. The social crisis of the Roman empire that began in the third century and accelerated in the two following centuries led to the impoverishment of great masses of people throughout the empire and to the accumulation of wealth in the hands of a few who for their part ruthlessly exploited those without property.[1] Because of this social reality that was reflected in its own composition the *Christian community* saw itself obliged to consider the relationship between rich and poor against the background of the claim to be a *community of equals* (see Gal. 3:28, 1 Cor. 12:13) and to strive to reach a solution that could prevent social differences and tensions becoming repeated within its own ranks and stop those who were discriminated against socially because of their poverty being neglected in the Church too. That poor people were humiliated twice over in this way is shown by James 2:1–4.

We can start from the fact that, especially since Paul's mission to the cities, well-off people also joined the Chrisitian movement and placed their *houses* at the disposal of the congregations that grew up as places where they could meet. However, they will not have been very numerous. In any case it would be wrong to see Christianity only as the religion of the lower orders. This is shown among other things by Pliny's letter to the emperor Trajan in the early second century in which he says that members of every social class were numbered among the Christians (*Ep.* 10:96:9). In other words the problems created by the coming together of different social classes within the congregation arose at an early stage. How this conflict was tackled theologically could be guided by one of *two biblical models*. On the one hand the Old Testament already contained *strong criticism of the rich* (for example, Amos 8:4-8, Isaiah 5:8-10 and 10:1-3, Sirach 34:24-27) which was continued in the New and further developed under the influence of the early Jewish spirituality of the poor (see Luke 4:16, 7:22, 16:13 and 19-31, Mark 4:19, 10:24, James 1:9-10, 2:5, 5:1-6). The high point is reached with Jesus calling the poor blessed (Luke 6:20). On the basis of this verse it was possible to ascribe preference to the poor in the matter of salvation. On the other hand there was the model of *using one's possessions to do good*. Here too the roots are to be found in Judaism (Prov. 3:27). It is to be found in Paul's letters (Rom. 12:13, 15:26, 2 Cor. 8:4) and in the synoptics (Matt. 6:3-4, 25:35-40, Luke 19:8). It was on the basis of these divergent ideas—renouncing possessions and using them for good works—that the *integration of rich and poor* had to be tackled. This was all the more imperative as the imminent expectation of the parousia gave way to coming to terms with living in the world and as the crisis of the Roman empire intensified. Since the Christian message of salvation in Jesus Christ applied to everyone because everyone stood in need of salvation, it was a question of winning the rich for the Church without neglecting the poor. Hence a *certain legitimation of property* was necessary. A certain unsavouriness always clung to the wealthy and their wealth in the Church, even if they were not promised heaven but were given a cry of woe. Tertullian expressed this in the pregnant formula: 'If heaven belongs to the poor it does not belong to the rich' (*Ux.* 2:8:5).

1. THE CHURCH BEFORE CONSTANTINE

(a) Theory

In two places in Acts (2:44-45, 4:32-37) the *community of goods* is described as an expression of the love based on Christ which the members of the community have for each other. The ideal of common ownership was also to be found in non-Christian philosophy.[2] It found its Christian justification in the letter of Barnabas (first half of the second century): 'If you share in that which is imperishable, how much more in those things that are perishable?' (*Barn.* 19:8, an argument echoed in *Didache* 4:8). Here what is called for is the renunciation of property for the benefit of others and in fact a *new attitude to property*. The argument is based not on the order of creation, though this is something we shall encounter later, but on pointing to sharing in the goods of salvation that have been won in Christ. This feeling of mutuality must not be exhausted in theological speculations but must be made actual in social life. The *Apology* of Aristides (around 125) presents a picture of the community that is replete with mutual solidarity and in which those who have give happily to those we have not (*Apol.* 15:7).

It seems likely that among Christians who had parted from their possessions for the sake of some good work one would find little understanding for those who clung on to their wealth. The *Shepherd of Hermas* (around 150) lays down that the rich are unfit for building up the Church because they are all tangled up in the world: it is only when they lose their wealth that they become useful (Vis. iii:6:5-7). Nevertheless in the community described in this work there are rich people who are living in luxury while others are in need. Salvation for the well-off can only result from them giving up their possessions (Vis. iii:9:2-6). Their goods, after all, are God's gift which is meant for all (Man. ii:4) and on which they have no exclusive claim. Poverty is an evil that threatens existence to the point that one is obliged to help the poor. Anyone who fails to do this burdens himself with blood-guilt (Sim. x:4:3). In the *Shepherd* we can see *the radical demand for the complete renunciation of possessions being watered down* to the demand to use one's possessions for the benefit of others. Whether those with possessions met at least this latter demand decided their affiliation to the Church.

We have already encountered *Tertullian's sharp criticism of the wealthy*. A similarly brusque impression is given by his characterisation of Christ as the one who always justifies the poor and condemns the rich in advance (*Pal.* 7). Tertullian also assumes the existence of a community of goods when he remarks that Christians have everything in common apart from their wives (*Apol.* 39). However, this statement would need to be interpreted as *an idealised picture* presented for the benefit of the non-Christian readership he was aiming at. This is suggested by the fact that in the same context he talks of everyone voluntarily contributing to the alms box. Clearly for him almsgiving was a form of renunciation of possessions which at least in intention corresponded to having everything in common.

In one of the empire's most prosperous cities, Alexandria, *Clement*, who died before 215 and was Tertullian's contemporary, developed a *doctrine of wealth* that was to be of fundamental importance for the further development of this subject. This he did in his treatise *What rich man shall be saved?* Apparently some rich people thought there was no place for them in the Church since, in keeping with Mark 10:25, the road was blocked for them (*Quis dives salvetur?* 2:2), and some members of the Christian community seem to have encouraged them in this view (*ibid.* 3:1). Clement uses an allegorical interpretation (*ibid.* 5) to combat a literal understanding of the story of the rich young man. Even the command to sell everything (Mark 10:21) is not to be taken literally: it is rather a question of not becoming subject to riches (*Quis dives* 11). *Wealth is morally indifferent* and it is the *use* that is made of it that determines whether it counts for good or evil (*ibid.* 14). The complete renunciation of one's possessions would mean that nothing at all was left for one to do good with (*ibid.* 13). This world's goods are a gift of God which are given to the possessor for the benefit of people in general so that he can let his brothers and sisters have a share in them (*ibid.* 16). Starting from these premises Clement develops a *classification of the relations between rich and poor.* The poor stand particularly in the love of Christ, and thus one should give to them of what one possesses in order to gain a heavenly reward (*ibid.* 31). In this way one can buy oneself one's eternal home in heaven (*ibid.* 32). The prayers of the poor are a means of assistance with God for the rich (*ibid.* 35). Clement deduces the duty of giving from the example of Christ. We have to imitate his love in our relations with our fellow men and women (*ibid.* 37). Clement thus succeeds in *legitimising private property while at the same time laying moral obligations on the owner of property.* He or she may not have to divest himself or herself of what he or she owns, but he or she must share it with those in need. The poor are not downgraded to mere recipients but are given an important mediatory role. In this way Clement did not call existing social relationships into question but was concerned to achieve a 'compromise of effective balance'[4] that bound rich and poor together through alms. This provided the framework for future discussion. While criticism of wealth that was unjust because it was used selfishly was retained, the rich were put under the obligation to use their wealth to help those in need and as it were to make this wealth legitimate.

(b) Practice

A useful illustration of this balance is to be found in the activity of *Cyprian of Carthage*, who died in 258. During the ten years he was bishop of Carthage a fairly rapid series of calamities necessitated the active help of the well-off:

the Decian persecution in 250, the plague from 252 to 254, incursions by nomads bent on plunder. Beyond this the effects of the empire's economic crisis were becoming more strongly noticeable. Cyprian wrote a short treatise on *alms-giving*. What is particularly remarkable about it is the high value attributed to alms-giving. Alms ensure salvation (*De eleemosynis* 1). Just as baptism wipes out one's old sins, so alms are capable of doing away with more recent ones (*ibid.* 2). Cyprian may be able to rely on earlier traditions (*2 Clement* 16:4; *Hermas, Sim.* ii: 5-10), but the urgency with which he recommends alms-giving as a means of atonement needs also to be understood as indicating that it was not easy to move those with wealth to give generously. Cyprian used biblical examples (*De eleemosynis* 4-8) in an effort to convince the well-off that they and their children would suffer no loss (*ibid.* 9-12). This could not arise if they allowed Christ to share in their wealth (*ibid.* 13). He mingled criticism and exhortation to urge them to exercise charity. In conclusion he pointed to the example of the community in Jerusalem. He then argued that everything that comes from God belongs to *all in common* and serves brotherly solidarity: hence the wealthy man who gives to others from his possessions is an imitator of God, inasmuch as he is allowing the order of creation to re-establish itself as it should (*ibid.* 25). In this way Cyprian justifies alms-giving not just with the argument from its effectiveness in wiping away sins but also from the common ownership of this world's goods intended by the creator. Nevertheless it cannot be denied that Cyprian *did not demand the complete renunciation of worldly goods* but merely, in what was probably a realistic assessment of the wealthy members of his congregation, their being given away for charitable ends.

Despite many difficulties in obtaining the financial means needed to support those in need, *the early Church's system of looking after the poor worked effectively.*[5] Money was raised by regular collections during services, by special contributions in emergencies, or by larger donations. It was a question of *voluntary giving*: an obligatory contribution on the lines of the Old Testament tithes was not practicable. The relief fund was controlled by the *bishop*. This increased his power and also his prestige among the non-Christian community (Cyprian *Ad Demetrianum* 10). The sometimes generous contributions to the churches made it possible to support substantial numbers of poor people: around 250, fifteen hundred widows and people in need were being provided for in Rome (Eusebius *Hist. eccl.* vi:43:11). Charitable activity found expression in visiting the sick, providing work and accommodating Christians on their travels.[6] In this way it offered members of the community a certain social security which among other things had the effect that beggars were unknown among Christians. However, with the exception of major disasters, *this welfare service was directed only at Christians*. In looking after the poor the pre-Constantinian Church had created a quasi-State organisation that looked after its members in a way that was not possible for the State. It was precisely this active help for the poor, which within the Church was seen as a major task, that *created one of the organisational pre-conditions for the Church's incorporation into the State under Constantine*. The Church had shown it was capable of building up an efficient system under the bishop's leadership in order to provide material aid. It had also given some first indications of how it might be possible to provide a *balance between social differences and contrasts*. For the most part it had succeeded in uniting rich and poor without major conflicts by calling on the former to show solidarity and to use their wealth for socially beneficial ends. The social status quo was not attacked, but its negative effects on the weakest members of society were softened, at least within the Church. Looking forward to the Church's subsequent attainment of a position of power in the Constantinian empire one could say that its efforts on behalf of the poor brought it the bonus of being trusted as the *protector of those no-one else respected*. On the basis of its theory the poor in the Church were not just the objects of other people's charitable activities but were on an equal level with the rich as free agents who received from the rich what God had bestowed on them. This theory found its most remarkable expression in the creation of the *order of widows*: one of the weakest sections of society became a respected class and thus contributed to the poor becoming independent agents.

(c) Conflicts

Even with regard to the relationship of rich and poor it was part of Christianity's earliest experience that *claim and reality did not always match up*. The cynicism expressed in the remarks about a brother's need recorded by James 2:16 and the lack of solidarity were well-known symptoms later.

Thus the *Shepherd of Hermas* tells us that rich people stayed away from the community because they were afraid they would be asked to give something (*Sim.* ix:20:2). They shunned public contact with other members of the community and preferred to associate with heathens (*Sim.* viii:9:1). Something that sounds like an everyday occurrence indicates a particular source of tension. The rich attempted to limit the community to the religious sphere and *not to live out comprehensively the implications of being a community*. For the author of the *Shepherd* this was an abandonment of the idea of community, about which there could be no half-measures. In addition there was the fact that because of their involvement in political and social duties the wealthy got mixed up with non-Christian practices (Tertullian *De idololatria* 18:21). They stood in particular danger of apostasy. Cyprian recorded after the Decian persecution that the rich were especially quick to fall away, and indeed the whole persecution had occurred because of spreading greed (*De lapsis* 5-6). In his view their wealth was more important to them than their salvation. In this context he had grave doubts whether the rich were at all suited for discipleship (*ibid.* 11-12), and after the persecution they were once again living in luxury (*ibid.* 30). We must accept that this kind of attitude on the part of wealthy Christians—lax in times of peace and unreliable in persecution—placed a heavy and permanent burden on relationships within the community. The community in Rome was split for among other things *social reasons* in 217 when the former slave Calixtus was elected bishop. Since 198 he had been responsible for administering the cemetery and organising relief for the poor. He was so successful in this that when it came to an election the choice fell on him and not on the well-educated Hippolytus. The latter's contacts extended as far as circles close to the emperor, and he moved among those with property. Calixtus's programme had a strong welfare stamp to it and looked forward to those with limited means having more influence in the community. The educated and the well-off joined Hippolytus in walking out. Only three decades later the same occurred in the dispute between Novatian, on the one hand, and his well-off adherents and, on the other, Cornelius. The social differences could result in the break-up of the community if other factors of a more or less theological nature were added to them, as later was to be the case with the Donatists too.

To *sum up*, it seems that the Church of the first three centuries had not established any finely honed theories to cover relations between rich and poor. It reacted to the situation it was faced with and tried to transplant the biblical message into a variety of contexts. It did not insist on everyone giving up his or her possessions but clung firmly to the view that possessions were a gift of God for the benefit of all. Wealth had to be shared with those who had nothing. The lack of solidarity that so often came in for criticism was to remain the problem during the centuries that followed.

2. THE ESTABLISHED CHURCH

(a) The Church in the State

The concept of the Constantinian turning-point suggests that it was *almost a new Church* that arose with the emperor Constantine. This is clearly *wrong*, for what made the Church attractive to the State had already been developed in the past and could now be used in the service of the State. *What was new was the favour shown to the Church* financially, legally and politically. The poor relief that had previously operated within the Church was now promoted by the State and seen as part of the State's social policy. The bishop, who had already been given the honorary title of 'father of the poor' (Jerome *Ep.* 52:6), became the protector of the poor and the exploited. The State too recognised this role[8] which had its origins in the Church's welfare activities before the fourth century. Ultimately the bishop was the only person who could still represent the *interests of the disadvantaged* over against corrupt officials and landlords bent on exploitation. The financial means needed for this came from *imperial donations* and especially also from *bequests*, which the Church was able to accept from 321 onwards. Skilful financial policies, already to a considerable extent in the hands of specially appointed stewards, increased the Church's landed wealth to the point that at the end of the Roman empire in the West it was among its largest landowners. This led to the danger that it would *side completely with the haves* and support their interests. Indeed, as far as slavery was concerned its attitude developed in this direction.[9] But as a rule it had a *different approach to the poor*, who included an ever larger section of the population. The *economic crisis* was escalating, thanks to a burden of taxation that had become almost insupportable and that was laid on the inhabitants of the empire to support the enormous expenses of the court and of maintaining the army and the administration, as well as inflation and the permanently unsettling effects of barbarian incursions. On the land numerous peasants sought protection from taxes with patrons, the possessors of enormous estates who were directly responsible to the governor and enjoyed fiscal autonomy. In any case for peasants who had formerly been free this meant that, since they often could not pay the rent, they became dependent on the landlords and were treated like slaves. If necessary private armies of thugs and corrupt courts ensured that the rich maintained the upper hand over the poor and rapaciously increased their holdings (Basil *Hom.* 7:5). In the cities, too, the number of poor people dependent on welfare was multiplying. In this way the excessive accumulation of wealth in the hands of a few rich people was contrasted with the progressive impoverishment of broad masses of the population. But it was not only the economic situation that had changed in the fourth and fifth centuries but also the *religious implications*: this was now happening in a society in which Christianity had become the *dominant religious power*. For the most part the exploiters and the exploited belonged to the same Christian community. Efforts to accumulate more and more wealth were the subject of sermons by Zeno, bishop of Verona from 363 to 372 (*Tract.* 15, 14, 21), and Basil the Great (*Hom.* 6). What they had to say about the lack of compassion shown by wealthy Christians indicates that Christian solidarity with the poor was flagging. Non-Christians, too, were noticing that *Christian claims were not being lived up to*. Ammianus Marcellinus commented ironically on the incident that took place at the papal election in 366 when a punch-up between supporters of the rival candidates, Damasus and Ursinus, led to a hundred and thirty-seven deaths. This kind of exertion was clearly worth while in view of the luxury and wealth to be expected. But he admitted that there were numerous provincial bishops who by contrast were models of good behaviour (*Res gestae* 27:3:11-15). It is no longer possible to judge whether the patriarch of Alexandria should be included here with his fleet of thirty ships whereby he controlled the corn trade with Constantinople.[10] It is not that bishops of this kind no longer gave alms but instead that they did so not so much as protectors and fathers of the poor but rather on the lines of the emperor graciously thinking of his people.[11]

In view of the unscrupulousness of the rich and the partial surrender of sections of the Church to their interests it is not surprising that there were *radical movements in opposition to this tendency*. Thus Eustathius of Sebaste (who died after 377) insisted that the rich had to separate themselves from their entire wealth if they wanted to find hope with God: he also encouraged slaves to flee. These teachings were condemned by the synod of Gangra.[12] The scandalous state of society came in for harsh criticism in the tract *On wealth* that came from Pelagian circles.[13] This argued against Clement of Alexandria's thesis that, if everyone gave up his or her property, nothing would be left for good works: 'Do away with wealth, and you will find no poor any longer. No one should possess more than he needs, and everyone will have what he needs. For a handful of rich people are the cause of many people's poverty.[14] Putting these ideas into practice would have meant a transformation of the existing system. What was signified by the voluntary renunciation of property by ascetics and monks was not a direct transformation of the system but its being insistently called into question. They showed that another way was possible than the exploitation of and contempt for the poor. Without their example the prophetic criticism of many bishops would have remained too distant from the reality. For there were also defenders of the poor who claimed the latter's rights from the rich.

(b) Defending the poor

There is hardly a preacher of the fourth and fifth centuries known to us who did not sharply criticise the exploitation of the poor and the luxury and greed of the rich, coupling a call to alms-giving with his criticism.[15] It was precisely in this age that the question of the justification of private property was raised once again.[16] *Ambrose of Milan* (339-397) reached the conclusion that God created everything for the benefit of everybody and that accordingly common use and common ownership corresponded to the order of creation, while private property arose from unlawful appropriation (*De officiis* 1:132). *Basil the Great* (ca. 330-379) emphasised that those with property are merely the stewards of their possessions. If they want to keep these exclusively to themselves they are guilty of theft, for the propertyless too had a claim on them. If everyone took only what he or she needed for sustenance, there would be neither rich nor poor (*Hom.* 6:7). In other words, 'he who loves his neighbour as himself possesses no more than his neighbour' (*Hom.* 7:1). However this criticism of private property was not directed at changing the existing state of affairs but rather at persuading the rich at least to ameliorate the misery of the poor through alms-giving. Basil sums this up by saying: 'It is not your theft that is condemned here but your refusal to share' (*Hom.* 6:8). Basil set up his own foundation for the sick and the poor with workshops, hostels and sick-bays. He used his own resources for this institution and moved the bishop's residence there (Gregory of Nazianzus *Or.* 43:63) in a clear gesture of solidarity. However, this was to lead on to the later pattern of institutional care which established those in need as a separate group beyond the pale. No less radical in his criticism of the wealthy was *John Chrysostom* (who died in 407). He faced his community in Constantinople with a bold plan for tackling poverty, adumbrated in the context of an interpretation of Acts 3:32-35. The community at Jerusalem had given an example of how inequalities should be overcome. Constantinople's Christian citizens should pool all their wealth to free the slaves, and there would be enough resources to feed everyone and no one would die of hunger. 'Have we not then made a heaven of earth?' John asked (*Hom. in Act.* 11:3). It is pointless to argue whether the preacher thought his plans could be realised. The text shows clearly the utopian potential that could be developed from this New Testament passage. *Confrontation with the biblical ideal* showed clearly that the world and its relationships were not as they should be.

3. CONCLUSION

No satisfactory answer can be given here to the *question why Christianity did not succeed in overcoming the injustices of society*. Too many factors were responsible. Christians were not immediately better than their non-Christian fellow-citizens. They too had fallen under the spell of the unnatural beast, as Basil called gold (*Hom. in Ps.* 14, 2:3). They did not see the face of the Lord in the poor (Gregory of Nyssa *Paup.* 1). Ambrose's exaggerated remark applied to them: 'A compassionate rich person is contrary to nature' (*In Luc.* 8:70). Even bishops and priests whose job it was to protect the poor had to realise they were helpless against rich people bent on exploitation. Many preferred to keep silent so as not to make the condition of the poor even worse (Salvian *De gubernatione Dei* iv:74-75, v:20-21). Certainly one of the achievements of Christianity was to have fixed in people's consciousness the idea that it was everyone's duty to relieve the distress of one's fellow human beings. *But it did not break the structures that led to impoverishment.* And the idea that the poor had a claim and a right to assistance disappeared more and more. Instead they became objects of solicitude.

If one is suspicious of the idea that the Church fell from grace with Constantine, one will conclude that Christian ideals and ideas did not show themselves to be strong enough to bring about social change with Christians as the potential agents of such change. Clearly those in particular who had a share in power and wealth did not believe the Christian message was capable of shaping a new reality. This underlines what Ambrose said in his commentary on the story of King Ahab and Naboth (1 Kings 21): 'Ahab is born anew every day and never vanishes from the world .... Every day Naboth is condemned, every day the poor man is struck down' (*De Nabuthe* 1:1).

If one could learn from history, then this would perhaps be the lesson in the present case: in view of the first world's emphasis on consumption and the way Christians are tied in to this system of increasing one's affluence, it would be illusory for Christians in the poor countries to hope for greater solidarity than that of alms. But his pessimistic conclusion does not take into account the liberating power of the word of God even and especially for rich Christians.

Translated by Robert Nowell

Notes

1. For the history of the later Roman empire the fundamental work is A.H.M. Jones *The Later Roman Empire, 284-602: a social, economic and administrative survey* (Oxford 1973) two volumes.
2. See M. Wacht, s.v. Gütergemeinschaft, *Reallexikon für Antike und Christentum* (Stuttgart 1984) XIII pp. 1-22.

3. See L.W. Countryman *The Rich Christian in the Church of the Early Empire* (New York 1980) p. 77.

4. M. Hengel *Eigentum und Reichtum in der frühen Kirche. Aspekte einer frühchristlichen Sozialgeschichte* (Stuttgart 1973) p. 65.

5. See on this W.D. Hauschild, s.v. Armenfürsorge II, *Theologische Real-Enzyklopädie* (1979) IV pp. 18-21.

6. Numerous instances are to be found in A. von Harnack *Die Mission und Ausbreitung des Christentums in den ersten drei Jahrhunderten* (Leipzig 1924) I, pp. 170-220.

7. See H. Gülzow *Christentum und Sklaverei in den ersten drei Jahrhunderten*, (Bonn 1969) pp. 146-172. L.W. Countryman, in the work cited in note 3 at pp. 155-157, suggests that the disputes described in 1 Clement should also be traced back to social conflicts.

8. See on this and on involvement in the State E. Herrman *Ecclesia in Re Publica. Die Entwicklung der Kirche von pseudostaatlicher zu staatlich inkorporierter Existenz* (Frankfurt 1980) pp. 205-348.

9. See the work cited in the previous note at pp. 256-257.

10. Cited by E. Herrmann, the work cited in note 8 at p. 303, note 123.

11. Thus rightly G. Uhlborn *Die christliche Liebesthätigkeit in der alten Kirche* (Stuttgart 1882), a collection of material that is still useful.

12. Mansi II:1099, 1110.

13. See on this H. Fischer *Die Schrift des Salvian von Marseille 'An die Kirche'. Eine historisch-theologische Untersuchung* (Frankfurt 1976) pp. 34-44.

14. Quoted from H. Fischer, the work cited in the previous note, p. 36.

15. A useful collection of sermons of this kind is provided by *Riches et pauvres dans l'église ancienne* ed. A. Hamman and S. Richter (Paris 1962).

16. See M. Wacht, the article cited in note 2, at pp. 36-52 (note 2), where there are numerous instances.

David Flood

Gospel Poverty and the Poor

LOTHAR OF Segni (†1216 as Innocent III) allowed himself a frank account of the *relations between the rich and the poor* in his *De contemptu mundi* (Poor, Sad World). Without entering on the particular problem of the whole text, we can take his dark portrayal of rich and poor as well observed if overdrawn. The man who has to beg rages against an unjust God for failing to distribute his goods fairly and against his stingy neighbour for failing to cover all his needs. The man in abundance works hard to get it and fears losing it. Tensions resulted from the evident disproportion in the enjoyment of life.

Famines such as occurred in the 1190s not only wreaked havoc among the populations of Western Europe. They made the fortunes of those who speculated in grains. The theologians, custodians of the age's consciousness, had problems with the poor masses around 1200. They affirmed the right of the poor to the extras of the rich. They acknowledged the footsteps of the naked Christ as the Christian way (*nudum Christum nudus sequi*). Yet they belonged very much to the agreements and practices within which the goods and advantages of this world circulated. One day, at a dramatic pass in his sermon, Peter of Poitiers (†1205) gave voice to the poor, pleading for the waste of a burdened table. He was preaching to clerics.

The *image of the poor Jesus* belonged to medieval culture. Saint Jerome's stark summary of the Christian way, *nudum Christum nudus sequere* (follow Christ bare), turned into a catch phrase of Christian commitment in the Middle Ages. Walter Map used the expression in his sardonic account of the Waldensians at the synod in Rome in 1179. James of Vitry used it in his 1215 life of Mary of Oignies (†1213) to designate her innermost longing.

Jesus' life with his apostles and the community of goods in Jerusalem served as models for life in common (*vita apostolica, ecclesiae primitivae forma*). The spirituality of the poor apostolic life waxed strong in the wake of the Gregorian reform (after Gregory VII, 1073-1085). In response to the Gospel, men and women lived poor lives preaching penance. James of Vitry and Thomas of Celano (Francis of Assisi's 1229 biographer) used the cultural tag *vita apostolica* to fix the Franciscan movement. The times of the Church's dominance in Western Europe, from the Gregorian reform until the emergence of the nation-states, laid special emphasis on the poverty of its saints.

In the *twelfth and thirteenth centuries*, following on a history of poor hermits and itinerant preachers, the Waldensians in Lyons, the Humiliati in Milan, and the Franciscans in Assisi banded together as Christians outside society's normal processes. They stand out in history as the foremost protagonists of the poor apostolic life. Peter Waldes abandoned his business and possessions and arranged for his family in 1173 upon hearing the story of Saint Alexis as well as passages from the Gospel (especially Matt. 19, 21—a passage to pin *nudum... sequi* to). He soon had followers, poor and apostolic, as well as trouble with the hierarchy. The Humiliati arose out of fraternities in Milan in the late twelfth century, finally clearing themselves with Rome as a religious association in 1201. Francis of Assisi left the world after ministering to lepers. Others gathered about him and from 1209 on they got along as a brotherhood.

To study the history of the movement of Gospel poverty in the late twelfth and early thirteenth centuries, we have to heed the following two points. First of all, we have to recognise the *limits and possibilities of the available evidence*. We do not have the means to trace the origins and purposes of Gospel poverty among the Waldensians and Humiliati. *Peter Waldes* and his brothers committed themselves as poor men to a life by the Gospel: they swore to it before Henry of Marcy and other Church dignitaries in Lyon in 1180. Bishops and brothers agreed on a culturally incontrovertible maxim. We have no way of finding out what that meant in practice, we do not know what the brothers did. Durand of Osca's *Liber antiheresis* explains the brothers ideologically. It engages in theological dispute, it does not report on Waldensian life. On the other hand, the sources for the history of *Franciscan poverty* are excellent. We even have the written agreement with which Francis and his brothers cleared their way through the confusions and challenges of their first years. (The sources for the poverty of the Dominicans cause no problem either. As teachers, however, they intended to correspond to the cultural ideal.)

The second point requires a longer argument than the present essay allows. It is not that the point is abstruse and wobbly, in need of much commentary and support, for it is simple and evident. The problem lies in the fact that it goes against the received teaching. Poverty plays no formal role in the initial Franciscan commitment. It enters into the history of the brotherhood when they have to contend with opposition and justify their way. *Poverty plays a role in early Franciscan life on the level of cultural legitimation but not on the level of practice.* When society sought to destroy the brothers by denying them meaning, they implied society had tried the same ploy on Jesus, whence his poverty. At that moment, they began using the word poverty, designating Jesus' condition, in fighting for their freedom.

In practical life, *Francis and his brothers were never poor.* Three clear qualities distinguished them from the poor of Assisi. One, they pursued a meaningful life vigorously and successfully, whereas the poor suffered society's relegation to passivity and meaninglessness. Two, they had work, both in the fields and workshops as well as in the poorhouses and leprosaria—where there was always work to do, however little recognised by Assisi.

Three, they had the assurance of life's basic goods, through the brotherhood and by their theory of mendicancy. By working with the traditional teaching on alms, they produced a theory which assured them access to a fair share of the available goods, and that in justice, not dependent on another's charity. The teachings on alms worked very differently when they served to justify a movement's claims rather than to assuage a rich Christian's conscience. The brothers were not poor save ideologically, as true and faithful Christians. They had left all to follow Jesus, and were doing quite well. Moreover, save on the level of cultural reference, they knew no one who was poor. They saw people in need, with a claim to succour and support. Franciscan history, by Francis' account, began in the acknowledgment of lepers as people, in conscious rejection of Assisi's laws of exclusion.

The sources for early Franciscan history as well as common sense combine to argue the purely ideological role of poverty in the life of the brothers. The primary source for early Franciscan history is the movement's basic document, read in the context of Assisian life (for which the sources are also good). Chapter Nine of the text arose as a theoretical defence of the movement against understandable social pressure. It contains the theory of mendicancy. It also assures the brother that the fraternity stands warrant for his basic needs. More to the point, it explains society's efforts to make them poor (to exclude them from life) by referring to Jesus' exclusion. It tells the brothers to embrace misunderstanding as a sign of their fidelity to the poor and humble Jesus. It puts a positive interpretation on a seemingly negative experience: the propertied world's dislike for the movement.

As for common sense, Francis and his brothers needed a sure material basis to survive. They turned from Assisi to dispose of their lives differently. In its own interests, as moral norm and legal force, Assisi could not admit their social heresy. It countered by seeking to remove them from its sight. If the brothers wanted to stay outside Assisi and live and thrive, they needed their own way of covering their needs. They had to have enough. They could not accept being poor in the world, for to be poor was to be dependent. And so they developed an *independent economics*. Then, in the face of social pressure, the brothers came up with a viable theory. For they could not expect legitimation from a system they had formally abjured.

When the Franciscans began winning more and more esteem as worthy men and women, society's spokesmen and propertied people had to recognise their legitimacy. They rapidly did so, but on their own terms. They had the cultural tools for the job. Francis was the perfect poor man, the Franciscans had recreated the life of the early Church. They were paragons of Christian virtue. The educated of that age held to those terms of explanation; they never saw the Franciscan movement in the terms of the early movement itself. They used the idea of the *vita apostolica* to make the movement a part of their world, as do historians today.

In 1182, a simple man of the people gave rise to the Capuciati in southern France. The fraternity promoted peace. It spread. At first it drew support. Then it provoked ferocious opposition and was squelched. It had questioned the rules of property and the exercise of political power. The judgment of heresy cleared the removal of the Capuciati. We know about them solely from the ones who condemned them as heretics. The Capuciati made some mistakes along the way, as did the Waldensians, for they did not survive in a Christian society. We cannot tell what mistakes, though, nor can we examine other aspects of their life, for we do not have the sources with which to reconstruct their history. For that reason, given the sources for early Franciscan history, we have to do as much with Francis and his brothers as we can, to clear up the story of medieval poverty. Critical Franciscan history honours the Capuciati and the Waldensians as well.

On the evidence of the early Franciscan writings, the Franciscan movement evolved outside the social agreements of civil life in the early thirteenth century. In their theory of mendicancy, the brothers stressed the cognitive divide between Assisi and the movement—precisely there where it was a question of access to material goods. There was no way in which the brothers could go along with the distribution of goods foreseen by such cities as Assisi. They put it cogently in the developed form of their basic document: *they intended to see to it that the good things of life got passed around among all.* (The case has been made in 'Assisi's Rules and People's Needs' in *Franziska-*

nische Studien 66(1984)91-104.) Francis' leper had more than a passing role in his story.

The brothers advanced very rapidly to the point where the Capuciati met their end. Their story then passed through a period of deep change whereby the *Franciscans ended up within the age's synthesis*: soon they enriched and enhanced the structures of medieval life, whereas initially they had challenged and shaken them. They ended up, and Francis in particular, the heroes of the cultural ideal of poverty. The Church pressed the interpretation, new recruits saw the movement in the terms of poverty and the apostolic life (the terms of Thomas of Celano's life of Francis in 1229), and the brotherhood subsided into a clerical order.

Before that happened, however, the movement had linked up with the Christian aspirations of the age in a foreseeable way. Since the Gregorian reform, Christians had sought a better grounding for their life in the world than supplied by the Church's regimentation. They picked up on the good news which Francis and his friends were circulating. *Enter the Penitents* as the natural audience for the Christian message of the simple Franciscans. (Penance: Christian fidelity as not commonly taught and practiced.) In bringing the Penitents into the history this way, we engage in social history and not in institutional history, and we use the best sources of the times to do it.

On the crest of the movement, around 1220, Francis addressed a message to the men and women attracted to the ways of his brothers and sisters. He began with a theory which justified and even demanded a life in penance. Then he detailed its practice, ending with a concise statement of the movement's ethos. He concluded by assuring his audience that the Spirit of the Lord visits men and women who live that way. (And therewith people had their explanation for the movement's so evident dynamism and joy in spite of its poverty—as society called the absence of wealth and social position.)

In the message Francis called for action: penance should make a difference in one's life. In the practice of the new fidelity, he emphasised the use to which goods should be put. It was a point which he returned to repeatedly, and most pointedly of all in his message to the rulers. In so far as lay people drew on Francis' ideas, they were bound to run into trouble with civic authorities. That happened, as the sources show.

The Penitents in Italy, as committed Christians, could count on some support from the Church authorities in Rome when they ran into trouble with municipal authorities. As a result we have papal bulls which stand up for the Penitents against the communes. In 1226 or 1227, Honorius III sent a message (*Ad audientiam nostram*) to the bishops of Italy. He told them to support the

Penitents in their laudable intentions against the 'potestates et rectores civitatum et locorum'—against the civic authorities. First however he described the Penitents and their trials. They were being forced to serve and fight for the commune. They were also being forced to support public life with their property rather than using it for other ends. What exactly was going on we cannot determine. It does centre on the social purposes of material goods. Gregory IX recalled this instruction of Honorius III to the bishops 26 May 1227 (*Nimis patenter*).

And in a letter to the Penitents themselves several days earlier (21 May 1227, *Detestanda humani generis*), Gregory IX strengthened their hand against the communal authorities as the Penitents had requested. More explicitly than in Honorius' letter to the bishops, Gregory's to the Penitents encourages *their use of goods for the alleviation of the needy*. The Penitents were using goods as Francis' message proposed, with the result that they had become embroiled with the ruling powers. They were disentangling themselves from the violence and harshness of communal ambitions. The use of goods by the rising merchant-banker class, spinning off ever larger numbers of poor people, proved more than many a Christian conscience could bear.

In the thorough reorganisation of Franciscan life in the 1220s, the Penitents lost the sort of support which Francis and his brothers had given them. Though they sought it, the politics of the clerical order differed sharply from the politics of the early movement. As professionals of religious poverty, the brothers taught the deceitfulness of riches while urging patience in the tribulations of this life. They had lost the proximity to the Penitents assured them by labour and service.

We can draw *two conclusions* from the preceding considerations on the movements of Gospel poverty in the late twelfth and early thirteenth centuries. First of all, the social action of the movements takes place within one set of terms; their cultural approval or condemnation unravels within another.

The *social action* arose out of daily life and addressed others in their material conditions. It made a difference in life, it challenged the social synthesis. Francis and his brothers said: Do peace, serve the needy, use your goods as God wills. And they said it with conviction and verve. It is too bad we cannot spell that out in the life of the first Waldensians.

The *interpretation* of the movements occurred within the age's culture. Having left all to follow Jesus, the Waldensians and the Franciscans faced a structured world. As innovators they necessarily had trouble with the interconnectedness and equilibrium of medieval life. They had to explain themselves, they had to submit to judgment. Even a prophet is historically tested, and his appeal to God alone does not suffice. The Waldensians and the

Franciscans got sanctioned and they got condemned for reasons other than their Gospel poverty. The reasons had to do with the repercussions of their actions and words among people. The new Christians had to work with forms and symbols, religion and ritual, with the administered consciousness of the age, in a way which fits their address to the practical problems of life.

And then, the people in the poverty movements were good news for the age's disadvantaged and needy. They raised the spirits of those excluded from and repressed by society. Women and beggars flocked to Robert of Arbrissel (†1117). According to the *propositum* of 1201, the Humiliati lived in peace and distributed among the poor whatever lay beyond their needs. In the early thirteenth century, many women used the poverty movement to break free of patriarchal property. The Penitents, drawing on the social discernment of the early Franciscan movement, sought to break the constricted circulation of goods sanctioned by communal politics. As long as the poverty movements continued to challenge the age's basic agreements, the brothers and sisters continued to mean good news from the weak and needy. When the Franciscans no longer lived in an inner tension with the structures sanctioned by God, although they remained theoretically poor, the weak and needy could expect more charity but hardly a change in their condition. They could not request food as upright men, on the terms of the early Franciscan movement's theory of mendicancy. The condition of the poor worsened as the Middle Ages drew to a close.

Michel Clévenot

'The Kingdom of God on Earth'? The Jesuit Reductions of Paraguay

AN ORIGINAL experiment, which was much discussed at the time and the implications of which are still debated, took place from 1609 to 1768 in the territory known then as Paraguay though it was much greater in extent than the present-day State of that name.

1. SOUTH AMERICA AFTER THE CONQUEST

To understand the field of reference of the events in question it is necessary to give a *short account of the situation of South America* (as is well known, the term 'Latin America' which resulted from the policies of Napoleon III is problematical) just after the Conquest.

From the demographic viewpoint, it is estimated that within fifty years one half or two thirds of the 'Indian' population succumbed to the onslaught of war, forced labour and especially the diseases imported by the Europeans. The official status of the occupied territories was the *encomienda*. In the King's name, the Indians were so to speak 'entrusted' to the colonisers, who were to look after them and *evangelise them*, but in exchange for a tribute. Since they had no money the Indians had to work in order to 'pay their debts . . . '.

Some missionaries protested against this legitimised exploitation. In 1511 the Dominican Montesinos delivered some fierce sermons on the subject at Hispaniola (Haïti). Las Casas took the matter up and in 1542 he secured the promulgation of the 'New Laws' which suppressed the *encomienda* and defined the system of the 'Two Kingdoms': that of the Spaniards and that of the Indians, both commonwealths being separately subject to the Spanish

70

monarch. Under this legal fiction, the Indians retained their laws and their chiefs, and paid the tribute as a sign of their subject status. But the *encomienda* system continued almost everywhere.

Religion, as it has been shown, is closely linked to politics. This was all the more so in South America inasmuch as the institution of the *patronato*, developed during the *Reconquista* against Islam, changed conquest into a holy war and officially entrusted the King with the evangelisation of subject peoples, delegating to him the power to appoint bishops on the spot. Because of the mediocrity of the Spanish secular clergy, it was the regular orders (Dominicans, Franciscans, Augustinians, Mercedarians and then Jesuits) who effected the missionary conquest and occupied the episcopal sees.

2. ORIGINS OF THE REDUCTIONS

The Spaniards arrived at the Plata estuary in 1516. *The conquest of the territory encountered tenacious resistance from the inhabitants*, the Guarani ('warriors'), belonging to the *tupi-guarani* tribal group which at that time occupied the greater part of the South American continent. These tribes lived in stone-age conditions, hunting, fishing, food-gathering and cultivating burnt land. They engaged in continual vendettas with neighbouring tribes and indulged in cannibalistic ceremonies. Their social organisation had a patriarchal basis; polygamy was a received practice; the men were concerned with war and hunting, and the women with food-gathering, sowing and harvesting. Their animist religion included a creator god and various spirits; shamans acted as intermediaries with the spirit world, curing sickness and presiding over ceremonies.

After the conquest phase, the *Spaniards settled down*. Their unions with local women produced half-caste children. In 1536 the town of Asuncion was established, and in 1587 three Jesuits founded a college there, and their preaching against the *encomienda* caused them difficulties. The Portuguese, however, who were masters of Brazil, also laid claim to control of the upper Parana region. In spite of Spain's annexation of Portugal in 1580, *bandeiras* from Sao Paulo were a dangerous threat to the Spanish settlements. In order to counter this danger, in 1607 Governor Hernandarias secured the constitution of the Jesuit 'Province' of 'Paraguay'. The provincial superior, Diego de Torrès, then decided to use a method which he had already tried out in Peru. He wished to regroup the Indians in villages isolated from the towns (Las Casas had already tried this in Guatemala, and Franciscans and Dominicans had done the same in several places). On 29 December 1609, near the junction of the Parana and Paraguay, the first reduction was founded— San Ignacio Guazù.

Why 'Reduction'? Because there Indians were 'inducted' (*reducti*) 'into civil life and the Church'. This kind of mission proved very successful. In 1630 there were *twenty-five Reductions comprising almost a hundred thousand Indians.* But the Sao Paulo *bandeiras* attacked them to obtain slaves. On two occasions, in 1631 and in 1637, the Jesuits had to organise an evacuation to the south in order to establish an area between the Parana and Uruguay which could be more easily defended. In 1640 they secured an authorisation to arm the Guarani (with firearms!) in order to defend themselves against the *bandeirantes,* who were defeated the year after.

Thereafter the Guarani 'State' experienced peace. Until . . . but this comes later.

3.   THE ORGANISATION OF THE REDUCTIONS

I shall not describe 'everyday life' in the Reductions in this article; that has been done elsewhere. Instead I shall concentrate on the basic elements of this very special form of organisation.

The most important feature was that the thirty-six Reductions of Paraguay were all built *on the same model.* All visitors noted this. To see one was to see all of them. This uniformity would seem to have been reinforced by the isolation which kept the Reductions apart from the surrounding world. No stranger, not even a Spaniard, apart from bishops and governors, had the right to enter them. The Jesuits conducted their experiment behind the shelter of a *virtual 'iron curtain'.* This tends to throw up the image of the concentration camps, but it is justifiable in terms of the extraordinary control exercised over space and time. The geometrical plan of the Reductions arranged the Indians' houses around the church and the Fathers' house from which they could survey everything and also remain aware of all that went on by means of a kind of benevolent espionage system. This was already something very much like the 'panoptic' system described by Jeremy Bentham in regard to prisons. The calendar was a kind of timetable which indicated what 'had to be done' for each hour of every day. When the bell rang you had to go to (daily) mass, to the offices, to meals, to work, or to recreation. The atmosphere might have been that of a monastery, or a Jesuit college. Might have been? No, it was. The punishment system was relatively moderate (whip and gaol but no death sentence) and is also reminiscent of the world of childhood.

In principle a Reduction was governed by an elected 'municipal council'. *In fact the two Jesuit 'parish priests' ran everything, with the help of Indian assistants*. The old tribal structure, with its 'caciques' and shamans, was completely superseded. The same is true of relations between age groups and the sexes (children went to lessons and women did household tasks and weaving; men saw to agriculture), and of rules of parenthood and marriage (monogamy, the individual family, each family in a separate household).

The *economy* is a special problem which is often discussed. Did the Jesuits establish communism? We must remember that the Guarani, hunters and nomads, did not have any form of individual land ownership, nor did they possess immovable goods. Rather, their burnt-ground establishments were communitarian in nature. The Jesuits wished immediately to 'give them a field, a house and reduce them to village life'. But alongside this private property (more a form of usufruct, since Spanish law treated the Indians as minors), most harvest and animal produce was stored in collective warehouses and controlled by the Fathers, who were in charge of redistribution. The primitive Christian community described in the Acts of the Apostles also experienced, as we know, problems of redistribution (see the episode of Ananias and Saphira, Acts 4:32-5, 11).

On examining external trade (very minimal and strictly controlled), military training (arranged by former officers among the Jesuits), dress (a kind of uniform for beforehand the Guarani had lived naked), hygiene (completely altered by the obligation to wear clothing, the reduction in bathing, and the change of diet), and religion (a rudimentary Christianity overlaid on beliefs and rites which remained effective), the same conclusion is to be reached throughout: *the Jesuits tried to impose another way of life on the Guarani.*

4.   THE PRINCIPLES OF THE JESUITS

This vast experiment was conducted on the basis of *quite explicit theological principles.*

The first, against which the Jansenists argued (see Pascal), consisted in the affirmation that, far from contradicting human nature, divine grace rendered it perfect. That is: *the best way to be a good Christian is to be a mature man.* But the Guarani, like all 'savages', were *not (yet) men but children.* Superior general Aguilar said expressly: 'The missionary has to be like the father of a family, for the Indian, whatever his age, is like a child in needing to be trained and punished for his own good.'

'Trained' or *'educated'—that was the central concept.* The pedagogical abilities of the Jesuits were now given free rein. For a century and a half the Paraguayan Reductions offered the astonishing model of Jesuit colleges

operating for a population of some 300,000 individuals. This was education in a vacuum, away from the 'contagion of bad example' and in accordance with criteria which were said to based on universal value judgments but were in fact European and Latin.

The second principle had to do with the Jesuit attitude to *politics*. They were educators of princes and confessors of monarchs, and everywhere they tried to *influence governments 'for the greater glory of God'*. Though in Paraguay they did not have the possibility and probably no desire to establish a State within a State, they seized the opportunity offered them to apply Christian morals on the scale of an entire country. Since Constantine, there is only too much evidence that ecclesiastics have dreamed of a form of 'Christian society'. There was all the more encouragement for Jesuits to think along these lines when their great theologian Francisco Suarez (1548-1617) stated: 'The Indian territories are sovereign States which are legally equivalent to Spain and entitled to be members of the universal community'. As against the abuses of colonisation, they claimed on behalf of the indigenous peoples the right to life, to freedom and to property. They therefore felt that they were charged with the duty of 'raising' the Guarani to the point of this ideal, which for them was the highest possible: that of being a good Christian: that is, a true Spaniard.

The excellent 'Jesuit-style' churches whose ruins are still to be seen in the territory of the former Reductions, bear witness to this 'acculturation', against which the Franciscan Jérôme de Mendieta had protested from the start of the conquest. The Jesuits, who were men of culture and the chambers of power, were wholly of one mind with the directive which the King of Spain gave to the Governor of Paraguay in 1609: 'These people are not to be deprived of their freedom but to be liberated from the dissolute ways and barbarism in which they lived'.

The Guarani, then, were 'barbarian' and 'dissolute' and therefore 'savages'. They lacked everything: civilisation, morality, the Gospel. They were 'impoverished', purely and simply. How could one not wish to 'liberate' them from this wretched state in order to allow them access to the inestimable riches of our fine European-Christian values? An overall conception of man and society, a whole way of looking at Christianity too, was at work in the Reductions.

5. INTERNAL AND EXTERNAL CONTRADICTIONS

But the 'Sacred Experiment', as it was sometimes known, came up against a *number of contradictions*.

Those thrown up by the system itself were not the most dangerous, for the almost total isolation of the 'Province' and the absolute control exercised by the Jesuits reduced the risks of explosion (which did occur, especially at the start).

The most *serious threats came from outside*. *Economically* speaking, the Reductions represented a serious malformation of the *encomienda* system. The colonials felt injured. *Politically*, the strategic situation of Paraguay on the frontier of Brazil was always a source of problems: first with the *bandeirantes*, then with the Portuguese settlers attracted by the effective spread of southern Brazil after the discovery of gold around 1700, then with the government of Portugal when it once again became independent in 1690. In respect of *religion*, the Jesuits were hardly without enemies, especially among the bishops, often Dominicans, who did not look favourably on the deliverance from their effective authority of some hundreds of thousands of faithful (whose numbers were intentionally underestimated). Even *in Rome*, the popes began to distrust these far too independent missionaries. The pontifical Congregation for the Propagation of the Faith was founded in 1622: henceforth it took charge of the direction of missions. In 1658 the Society of Foreign Missions was established in Paris, and began to compete with the Jesuits, especially in China.

Times changed. The Society of Jesus, precisely because of its influence and success, provoked the establishment of a powerful coalition ranged against it. The spirit of the 'Enlightenment' became influential among European intellectuals and spread in royal circles. Whereas Montesquieu and even Voltaire had admired the Paraguay experiment, now libellous rumours reached attentive ears.

Then the Jesuits fell into a trap. In 1750, by the Treaty of Madrid, Spain exchanged with Portugal the colony of Sacramento on the Plata for seven Reductions located in the south of Uruguay. If the Jesuits accepted this arrangement they would lose the trust of the Guarani who were forced to surrender their best land to the greed of Portuguese settlers; if they refused to accept the terms of the Treaty, they would be in a state of rebellion against their Kings. Superior General Visconti ordered them to accept the exchange. Most Jesuits obeyed. But the Guarani put up a resistance with the firearms which they had. The 'Guaranitic war' lasted for several years. Finally, Spanish and Portuguese troops put an end to it.

The Portuguese Prime Minister, the Marquis of Pombal, who was a sworn enemy of the Jesuits, used this pretext to expel the Jesuits from Portugal and its colonies (1759). The King of Spain followed suit in 1767 (France had anticipated him in 1762). The missionaries were shipped out from Buenos-

Aires like convicts. Many of them died in prison or in exile. On 21 July 1773 Pope Clement XIV suppressed the Society of Jesus.

The Reductions of Paraguay were laid waste and looted. The Guarani were reduced to slavery or took refuge in the forests. *The only survivor of the disaster was the Guarani language*, for which the Franciscans and Jesuits had written grammars and dictionaries, and which is now the official language of Paraguay. It is the only example of this kind in the whole of America.

6. THE HISTORY OF THE STORY

Many words have been written on the history of the Jesuit province of Paraguay. The debate has been obfuscated by supporters and opponents, and by interpreters of all kinds. Among the questions most often raised, the following deserve special mention: Did the Reductions constitute an actual Jesuit State, independent of the Spanish Crown?—Did the Jesuits found a communist system, defined by the collective ownership of the means of production?—Or did they try instead to establish a perfect society within the bosom of a corrupt world?—Did their action comprise the transformation of a society without any State into a totalitarian and police State?—Finally, is it not true to say that they quite straightforwardly knew how to adapt themselves to circumstances, following a pragmatic policy which simultaneously answered their desire to educate and evangelise, the demands of Spanish legislation (which they had often inspired), and the needs of the Guarani people? . . .

I hope that this account will allow this kind of question to be answered. Therefore I should like to conclude by asking yet another: Did not the Jesuits in fact fail where they hoped to succeed, and succeed where they laid least emphasis? The experiment of the Reductions seems in fact to have been a typically 'colonialist' action. It consisted in exporting a European model of civilisation and in imposing it as the best possible, without taking into account the fact that it inexorably destroyed the structure proper to those to whom it was applied. Was this Europeocentrism? Yes indeed. But more exactly it was the result of a certain Western vision of reason and faith which too hastily baptized as 'universal' phenomena which were entirely contingent. Montaigne saw 'savages' brought from America put on show. He argued thus: 'The laws of conscience, which we say arise from nature, arise from custom. Each person, inwardly respecting the habits and opinions which are approved and received roundabout him or her, cannot but depart from them with remorse, nor obey them without approval.... Hence that which is outside the framework of custom is considered to be outside the bounds of reason; God knows how unreasonably that occurs most often!' (*Essays* Book I, ch. 22).

Paradoxically, in failing to change the Guarani into Spaniards, perhaps the Jesuits won a victory which they did not expect. They enabled a people to preserve their language: that is, the very crucible of its personality, the best means of recovering its identity one day. Long live free Paraguay!

Translated by J.G. Cumming

BIBLIOGRAPHY

Sources

P. Hernandez S J. *Organicación social des las doctrinas guaranies de la Compañía de Jesús* 2 vols (Barcelona 1913).
P. Pastells S J. *Historia de la Compañía de Jesús en la Provincia del Paraguay* 4 vols (Madrid 1912-23).
L.A. Muratori *Il Cristianesimo felice nelle missioni dei padri della compagnia di Gesù* (Venice 1743) translated into French by P. Laurmel SJ *Relation des missions de Paraguay* (Paris 1983).

Studies

A. Armani *Città di Dio e Città del Sole. Lo 'Stato' gesuita dei Guarani (1609-1768)* (Rome 1977).
A. Metraux *La Religion des Tupinamba et ses rapports avec celle des autres tribus Tupi-Guarani* (Paris 1928).
A. Metraux 'Le Caractère de la conquête jésuitique' *Acta Americana* I No. I pp. 69-82 (Austin 1943).
M. Mörner *The Political and Economic Activities of the Jesuits in the La Plata Region. The Hapsburg Era* (Stockholm 1953).
M. Haubert *La Vie quotidienne au Paraguay sous les Jésuites* (Paris 1967).

Part IV

Irruption of the Poor—Evangelical Challenge to the Rich

Norbert Greinacher

Liberation Theology in the 'First World'?

THOSE RESPONSIBLE for this issue of *Concilium* asked me to write an article entitled 'Liberation Theology in the "First World"'. I deliberately put a *question mark* behind this title since, the longer I thought about it, the more problematical the whole concept became.

It it well known that liberation theology arose in Latin America in a very particular socio-economic context that was, and still is, characterised above all by exploitation and repression. Liberation theology was, and is, the creative, authentic attempt to give a genuinely Christian answer to this situation of real suffering.

Now I do not at all deny that there is exploitation and repression in the 'First World'. I shall return to this subject. But it seems to me to be inadequate, even presumptuous, simply to transpose this theology, wrung from suffering, into the 'First World'. It is inadequate because we of the 'First World' live in a different socio-economic context, and liberation theology rightly insists that *theology must be contextual*. It is presumptuous because we 'First World' theologians and Christians generally live in a totally different and by comparison privileged position.

Then there is also an important difference (among many others) between liberation theology in the 'Third World' and in the 'First': the theology of the affluent North may not, and cannot, turn a blind eye to the development of freedom in modern times, nor to the Enlightenment—whatever this may imply in detail—without retreating from the field of public and scientific discourse. It may not, nor can it, prescind from the 'Enlightenment dialectic' without renouncing the claim to be contextual theology. Clodovis Boff has rightly drawn attention to this difference of situation between Latin America and Europe.[1]

In saying this I do not in any way wish to put forward a simplistic division of labour in theology and the Church, as if Christians in Latin America are to concern themselves with the poor, and Christians in the 'First World' with the rich. If Christians in the 'First World' refuse to respond to the appeals, challenges and options presented by Christians in the 'Third World', they damage their own understanding of themselves as part of the one, universal Church, and such action would reveal them to be *schismatics, forsaking the unity of the Church.* 'If one member suffers, all suffer together; if one member is honoured, all rejoice together' (1 Cor. 12:26). The fundamental option in favour of the poor, most notably proclaimed at the general assembly of Latin American Bishops in Puebla in 1979, is something that applies to the whole Church. Furthermore, the 'dispute over liberation theology'[2] is not only a matter for liberation theologians: it concerns all theologians and the whole Church. Not only because it calls for solidarity, requiring 'First World' theologians to stand by their browbeaten colleagues in the 'Third World' with words and deeds (far more than they have done so far), but first and foremost because the issue involves fundamental questions of theology and Church life.

If we advocate a contextual theology as something both legitimate and necessary, we shall not—to be consistent—put forward a 'First World' liberation theology. We still have to learn, particularly in the Catholic Church, that there is no such thing as a single, universal and universally acknowledged theology. Nowadays, much more than heretofore, we have to reckon with a *multiplicity of theologies.* If Ernst Käsemann can speak of different theologies within the New Testament itself, how much more must there be a multiplicity of contextual theologies today, once more expressing the fact that God cannot be the object of exhaustive reflection and conceptualisation, and that theology is never more than an approximation, necessarily shaped by the particular historical and social situation, albeit this multiform phenomenon is always related to the same absolute mystery which we call God.

Having said this, however, I am committed to the view that 'First World' theologians have to implement a prophetic and political theology that very seriously takes account of the challenge posed by liberation theology, reflecting upon God and the 'First World' in terms of the fundamental option for the poor. I would regard this as involving a critical dialogue between different theologies—an absolute necessity—including reciprocal 'fraternal correction'.

In what follows I shall attempt to outline a number of what I regard as important elements of a *prophetic and political theology* in the 'First World'.[3]

THE WORK OF SORROW

First of all, Christian theology in the 'First World' will have to consider very deeply *how much guilt it must bear*, within the history of Western theology, for the four dangerous diseases which afflict world society today and which actually threaten its continued existence, namely, the East-West conflict, the North-South conflict, the ecological crisis and the man-woman conflict— which all overlap to some extent. I am aware that it is a matter of dispute whether and how far Christianity is involved here, and at present I cannot enter into this discussion. But I am convinced that, if there is to be a prophetic and political theology in the 'First World', theology must first take on the *work of sorrow*—in biblical terms, there must be repentance. I at any rate find the greatest challenge to my Christian faith in the fact that the history of the last five hundred years in Latin America has been determined largely by Christians and the Catholic Church, and the 'result' of this period is a structural social injustice that cries to heaven.

AGAINST NEO-COLONIALISM

Such a *metanoia* in the way the history of theology and the Church is assimilated must lead not only to opposition to all forms of political and economic neo-colonialism (we shall speak of this later on), but also to allowing the *Church and theology in the 'Third World' to enjoy their own freedom.* Primarily since the 2nd General Assembly of Latin American Bishops in Medellin in 1968, both Church and theology in Latin America have started out on this path of emancipation, and it is the absolute Christian duty of the universal Church authorities in Rome, and of the churches and theologians of the 'First World', not only to refrain from in any way obstructing 'Third World' Christians from following this path, but actually to use all their means to promote this process towards autonomy, in the same way that good parents know that they have to help their children to become independent of them, however painful it may be.

At the *theoretical level* this means recognising a special 'Third World' theological path which is equally faithful to the Judeao-Christian tradition that is binding on all Christians. At the *practical level* it means recognising new pastoral methods and initiatives. It applies at the financial level too: financial help must be given without any strings attached.

We must realize, furthermore, that parents must also learn from their children, i.e., in this case, the Christians of the 'First World' have to learn from the theory and practice of Christian living in the 'Third World'. By way of illustration I will cite something that has given me much pause for thought. In the preface to the German edition of the catechism of the Peruvian *campesinos Vamos caminando*[4], Bishop J. Dammert of Cajamarca writes this: 'The Catholic books used in Latin America were European . . . [Now] we have the book *Vamos caminando* which is travelling in the opposite direction. It is offered to Christians in the old land of Germany, which is so full of theological literature.'[5]

AGAINST 'CONSUMISMO'

A 'First World' theology that allows itself to be challenged by liberation theology will have to offer a critique of the operative values of one-sided consumerism, *consumismo*. Pier Paolo Pasolini has given an impressive analysis of this destruction of the culture of the individual by the consumer society.[6] He writes: 'Consumer pressure is the pressure to obey an unuttered command. Everyone . . . is subject to the dishonouring pressure to be like the others, whether in matters of consumption, happiness, or freedom. That is the command he has been given, that he "must" obey, if he is not to feel an outsider. Being different from others was never as difficult as it is in our age of tolerance.'[7]

ALIENATION THROUGH AFFLUENCE

In his *Philosophical and Economic manuscripts* Karl Marx described the growing alienation of the labourer as a result of increasing poverty: 'The labourer becomes poorer, the more wealth he produces, the more power and scope his production acquires. The labourer becomes a cheaper commodity, the more commodities he produces. The exploitation of the world of human beings increases in proportion to the exploitation of the world of things.'[8] As we shall see, the 'First World' is still acquainted—as in Marx's time—with the *alienation that comes from poverty*, but there is also the specific *alienation through affluence*, i.e., man's enslavement to the fetish of prestige, income, possessions, property and achievement.

This means that Christian theologians must beware of making poverty and the poor into an ideology, which, throughout the history of Christianity, has often enough been bolstered by a misinterpretation of Jesus' 'You always have the poor with you' (Matt. 26:11). The real task is to overcome both alienation through poverty and alienation through affluence.

A NEW LIFE-STYLE

For very many 'First World' Christians (who are mostly very rich, at least measured by the poverty of the 'Third World') this will not be possible without a radical transformation of the life-style of the individual, the family, the Church community, and society itself. As early as ten years ago, in connection with the 4th United Nations Conference on Trade and Development (UNC-TAD·IV), the two Christian churches in the Federal Republic of Germany produced this statement:

> For some time now people of diverse world-views have been trying to find and implement a 'new life-style', in which a central feature would be the jettisoning of consumer habits and tendencies which hitherto have been accepted as the norm ... A simple style of life in the industralised countries is intended to promote a more just distribution of those of this world's goods which, for physical or economic reasons, are in short supply. However, practical action of this kind goes beyond renunciation and aims at a changed attitude, a new way of treating fellow human beings, time, money and things.[9]

CRITIQUE OF CAPITALISM

But as well as transforming their life-style, Christians in the 'First World' will have to subject the capitalist economic system to a radical critique on the basis of the Judaeo-Christian tradition. It is well known how severely this system was criticised in the concluding document of the 3rd General Assembly of Latin American Bishops in Puebla in 1979: 'The free market economy in its purest form, which still prevails in our continent and is legitimised by certain liberal ideologies, has increased the gap between rich and poor by placing capital before work, economic interests before social considerations. Minority groups, sometimes in league with foreign interests, have used the opportunities presented to them by these superannuated forms of the free market to secure their own advantage at the expense of the greater part of the population' (no.47).

This critique of capitalist economics, however, applies not only to Latin America but also the the 'First World'. The Catholic bishops of Canada[10] and the USA[11] have largely adopted this critique. Theology in the 'First World' has the urgent task of substantiating this critique even more and rendering it more convincing, in the face of considerable resistance on the part of society.

OPTION FOR THE POOR

The same applies to the 'preferential option for the poor' which was so convincingly called for in the concluding Puebla document[12]: it concerns not only the Church in Latin America, but also the churches in the 'First World'. And no one will have the temerity to say that there are no poor here. According to reliable estimates by the German Caritas Association, in 1985 in the Federal Republic there were 2.5 million recipients of social assistance and about 650,000 people receiving unemployment assistance.[13] Adding on those who through reticence or ignorance fail to apply for assistance, those who have dropped through the unemployment assistance net or whose income (salary, wage or pension) does not come within the scope of social assistance, we can assume that *about 10 per cent of the population of the Federal Republic are poor*, relatively speaking.[14] The credibility of Christians, church communities, theologians and churches in the 'First World' will depend on whether, like the Christians in the 'Third World', they show solidarity with their own poor.

CRITIQUE OF DEVELOPMENT AID

However, 'First World' Christians must not restrict their expression of solidarity to the poor of their own countries, but also extend it to the poor of the 'Third World'. In doing so they will have to subject the traditional development aid (both State and private) to a very critical analysis. Too often this so-called 'development aid' serves the economic interests and expansion-ism of donor economies and enterprises, is tied to political or economic conditions, or simply functions as an export channel.

Furthermore the criticism that *development aid can be counter-productive* in many cases, particularly in the middle and long term, must be taken very seriously.[15] Each case must be examined in detail to see whether such aid really benefits the poor and tackles their basic needs, or merely promotes the growing wealth of a 'bridgehead élite' in 'Third World' countries.

THEORY OF DEPENDENCE

'First World' Christians must not close their minds to the bitter insights of the theory of dependence which liberation theologians have largely made their own. Pope John Paul II also identified himself with the central feature of this theory when, in his inaugural address at Puebla, he spoke of the 'mechanisms which, since they are stamped by materialism and not by an authentic humanism, make the rich even richer at an international level, at the expense of the poor, who became even poorer.'[16]

The fact that 'First World' Christians are themselves oppressors has yet to come home to them. On the international plane, the peoples of the 'First World' are the oppressors of those of the 'Third World'. We are so rich because people in the 'Third World' are so poor. We are often so fat because the others are starving.

THE WORK OF SOLIDARITY

In order to achieve this change of awareness in people in the 'First World', *practical action for solidarity* is often very important. What I mean by this is action on the part of individual Christians, solidarity groups and Church communities, who not only provide information but give very concrete support to projects in 'Third World' countries. Not only does such help benefit people directly: at least equally importantly, it disseminates information; Christians and 'basic communities' show others what being Christian means in practical terms. It often happens, as a result of partnerships between church communities here and 'basic communities' overseas, that the Church community at home has been significantly changed by having had to deal in practical terms with the experience of the North-South conflict.

CRITIQUE OF THE WORLD ECONOMIC SYSTEM

Furthermore, however, it is an important task of a prophetic and political theology to draw attention to the injustice, the structural sinfulness of the existing world economic system. In a world population of roughly five thousand million there are today about eight hundred million suffering from undernourishment, the lack of health care, high infant mortality, low life-expectancy and inhuman environmental conditions. The 'war of starvation' between the rich Northern lands and the poor lands of the South claims about eighty million dead every year, far more than the Second World War claimed in more than five years.

The 'First World' scarcely takes any notice of this gigantic, planetary human catastrophe, although there can be no doubt that serious efforts could avert it.

Basically, the so-called 'world economic order' is nothing but the *classical bourgeois property individualism and property egoism of the eighteenth and nineteenth centuries, projected on to the relationship between the possessors (the 'haves') and the poor nations within a world context.* Today the 'haves' still stress their right to property, i.e., to their standard of living, and insist that the nations of the 'Third World', who live below the subsistence level, acknowledge this 'right' to property. To that extent today's world economic order and its ideological defence is only a developed expression of the bourgeois ideology of the eighteenth and nineteenth centuries. The nineteenth and twentieth century exploitation of workers by the owners at a national level is now being applied worldwide in the exploitation of people in the 'Third' and 'Fourth' worlds by those of the 'First' and 'Second'. This was clearly expressed by President Julius Nyerere in a lecture given in Bonn, in the middle of May, 1985, to the Friedrich Ebert Trust: 'The transfer of wealth from the poor to the rich, which characterises the present system of trade and finance, is immoral. It is just as immoral on the international scale as it is within nations ... No one who believes in God, or even simply in humanity, can any longer accept this drain of resources from the poor to the rich countries.'[17]

There can be no ethical justification for the rich lands of the North involving the poor lands of the South in *ever greater financial dependence.* It is a scandal that the 'Third World' countries' mountain of debt has by now reached a billion dollars, by which primarily North American and European banks profit through their high interest rates.[18] It is a catastrophe that in 1984 the countries of the 'Third World' paid 17 thousand million DM (Deutsch Marks)—in interest and repayments—more than they received in development aid in the same year. In 1985 the Latin American countries alone paid 100 thousand million dollars, in interest and repayments, to the rich Northern countries. It is immoral for the government of the USA to pass on its own budget deficit of around 150 thousand million dollars and its balance of trade deficit of around 135 thousand million dolars (estimate for 1985) to other countries by a high interest policy, primarily at the expense of the world's poor.

Furthermore, there is a *close connection between the North-South conflict and the East-West conflict.* A great number of the 159 wars that have been waged worldwide since 1945, of which 22 have lasted for more than five years, are so-called 'representative wars' waged by nations in the interests of the great powers.[19] The national efforts of small nations to gain self-determination and social justice are again and again subsumed by the great powers into the East-West conflict and subordinated to their imperialist interests.

But at a purely pragmatic level there is a connection between the East-West conflict (which has already become an anachronism) and the North-South conflict, in that all the financial resources, research investment and economic productivity that are put into *armaments* are thereby denied to the world's poor. It is a scandal that, in 1984, a billion dollars were spent on armaments, whereas in the same year only 350 thousand million were set aside by central governments for development aid.[20] Willy Brandt is right when he says, in his book *Der organisierte Wahnsinn* [Organised Madness]: 'The one billion dollars that were spent this year throughout the world on armaments spell death for millions of our fellow men. The means that would allow them to live are absorbed by weapons.'[21] Giovanni Cheli, the Vatican's ambassador to the United Nations, has put it similarly: 'Even if they are never used, these weapons, because of their high cost, kill the poor or allow them to die of starvation.'[22] There can be no moral justification for the estimated 70 thousand million dollars being spent on the 'Strategic Defense Initiative' (SDI) up to 1994, at present levels.[23] It is a crime against the poor of the world.

As early as 1982 the armaments industry became the chief consumer of the resources it claims to protect.[24] Between 50 and 100 million people are directly or indirectly occupied in military tasks. More than 500,000 experts work in military research. Every year 35 thousand million dollars are spent on developing new weapon technologies. The armed forces of all countries swallow up 6% of world oil production and more aluminium, copper, nickel and platinum than Africa and Latin America together use for civilian purposes. Over the whole world there are more soldiers in uniform than teachers. More money is spent on military research than on research into new sources of energy, medical research, agricultural research and environmental conservation together. The USA spends more money on modernising small military rockets than the World Health Organisation spent in 10 years on successfully eliminating smallpox (100 million dollars).

In other words, human beings must starve by the million because we are so equipped with armaments. Every Christian woman and man must find this situation intolerable. The champions of a prophetic and political theology, following Jesus of Nazareth, will tirelessly draw attention to this intolerable situation and do all in their power—including personal involvement—to effect a change.

Translated by Graham Harrison

Notes

1. N. Greinacher/C. Boff *Umkehr und Neubeginn* (Fribourg, Switzerland 1986) pp. 50f.

2. See my book *Konflikt um die Theologie der Befreiung* (Zurich 1985).

3. See N. Greinacher *Der Schrei nach Gerechtigkeit. Elemente einer prophetischen politischen Theologie* (Munich 1986).

4. Fribourg, Switzerland 3 1983.

5. *Ibid.* xiii.

6. P.P. Pasolini *Freibeuter-Schriften. Die Zerstörung der Kultur des Einzelnen durch die Gesellschaft. Quarthefte* 96 (Berlin 1978).

7. *Ibid* p. 37.

8. K. Marx/F. Engels *Werke*, supplement I (Berlin 1973) p. 511.

9. H. Kunst/H. Tenhumberg *Soziale Gerechtigkeit und internationale Wirtschaftsordnung* (Munich 1976) p. 27.

10. 'Ethical Reflections on the Economic Crisis', The Catholic Bishops' New Year Statement, 1983, written by the Episcopal Commission on Social Affairs, Canadian Conference of Bishops. Extensive excerpts are to be found in *The Globe and Mail* 1 January 1983, p.T 15.

11. 'Die Armen müssen Massstab sein' (together with the first draft of the pastoral letter of the USA Catholic Bishops). *Publik-Forum Dokumentation* (Frankfurt, n.d.). For the actual statement of the USA Catholic bishops, see *Origins* 14 No. 22/23 (1984).

12. See chiefly nos. 1134-1165.

13. *Caritas aktuell* no. 3 (1985).

14. On the question of structural poverty, see particularly: S. Leibfried & F. Tennstedt *Politik der Armut* (Frankfurt 1985); K.M. Bolte & S. Hradl *Soziale Ungleichheit in der Bundesrepublik Deutschland* (Opladen 1984); G. Schäuble *Theorien, Definitionen und Bewertung der Armut* (Berlin 1984); *Soziale Ungleichheiten* ed. R. Kreckel (Göttingen 1983).

15. E.g. B. Erler *Tödliche Hilfe. Bericht von meiner letzten Dienstreise in Sachen Entwicklungshilfe* (Freiburg 1985).

16. *Predigten und Ansprachen von Papst Johannes Paul II. bei seiner Reise in die Dominikanische Republik und nach Mexico. Verlautbarungen des Apostolischen Stuhls* 5 (Bonn 1979) pp. 48-67 (63) (Sermons and discourses of Pope John Paul II during his visit to the Dominican Republic and Mexico, 1979).

17. *Frankfurter Rundschau* 1.8.1985.

18. *Die Zeit* 3.1.1986.

19. *Frankfurter Rundschau* 5.10.1985.

20. *Frankfurter Rundschau* 29.5.1985.

21. Cologne 1985.

22. Quoted from *Das Evangelium des Friedens* (Munich 1982) ed. P. Eicher p. 190.

23. *Vorwärts* 26.10.1985.

24. *Frankfurter Rundschau* 27.3.1982.

Enrique Dussel

The Ebb and Flow of the Gospel

I HAVE been asked to comment on the *missionary aspect of the challenge posed to the rich churches by the poor ones*. This involves a 'theology of mission' which here I can only suggest, open up, provide some pointers to.

We have recently gone through different stages in the history of mission theology.[1] The churches have discovered that mission touches on the essence of the *ecclesia*, that going out *ad gentes* is founded on the command that brought the first communities into being: 'Go and make disciples of all nations' (Matt. 28:19).[2] The Gospel goes out from a spiritual 'centre' to the 'periphery'—so the 'going to' the pagans can be called the *'ebb'* of the message. The second stage is like a *'flow'* of the Gospel: the evangelised become the evangelisers and the 'mother' churches of the centre find a missionary challenge coming from the 'new' churches on the periphery. This 'flow' is not the first one in history, but today it is taking on special characteristics which I should like to comment on.

1. THE EBB OF THE GOSPEL TOWARDS THE PERIPHERY

Clearly, the *Gospel started from Israel, from Jerusalem at Pentecost*, when Peter began speaking and the conversion of pilgrims who had come to the holy city started: 'Men of Judaea, and all you who live in Jerusalem . . . ' (Acts-*Praxis* 2:14);[3] when the 'utopian community' (2:42-7) was born; when Philip set out (8:4ff), when Peter began his work (10:1ff); and the Gospel spread to the pagans through 'persecution'—not through a secretariat or congregation (11:19). Paul too was sent out to bring 'the Good News from God to the pagans' (Rom. 15:16). This 'centripetal' movement is also expressed well in Jesus' saying that 'salvation comes from the Jews' (John 4:22).

91

In the same way, through means that we know little about, the Gospel reached *Ireland* between the fourth and fifth centuries in the hands of monks who organised a flourishing Christianity in the 'island of saints', peripheral to the Christianity of mainland Europe.

From the fifteenth century onwards, Latin-Germanic Christianity, that of Western Europe, thanks originally to Spain and Portugal, then to Holland, France and England, and finally to the United States[4], set out on the process of *evangelising the Third World*. This was a new centripetal movement, this time from North to South;

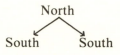

These Christians went out influenced by their certainty of their 'civilising superiority' over other nations. So the whole world came to be plundered by Europe and the United States, ending with Africa, where the 'missionary' eyes of David Livingstone (*Missionary Travels and Researches*, 1857) opened the horizons of the continent to the greed of companies exploiting the resources of the poor countries. Europe and the United States, for their part, *confused being Christian with being developed and technologically superior*. Let us take an example from the first American Catholic Missionary Congress: 'I am convinced as a man who has been privileged to visit all the countries of Europe, many of Asia and Africa and the entire Orient, that there is no such Catholicity (as ours ...) the most generous, the most charitable, the most whole-souled on the face of the earth. In other words, they are in reality ideal Catholics here, and I cannot believe that when American Catholics learn of the great needs of our Holy Mother Church in far-distant possessions (!), they will turn a deaf ear to their needs and necessities'.[5] There is no need to give further examples of the spirit of spiritual 'superiority' which filled the missionaries all the churches sent to the Third World, where, in the name of 'Christendom', Latin and Germanic Catholics, Protestants from the older churches and followers of new sects, all confused the Gospel with their own culture.

2.   THE 'FLOW' OF THE GOSPEL TOWARDS THE CENTRE

Just as the waters of the sea ebb from the land and flow back on to it, so the Gospel flows back towards the centre in a process of re-evagelisation. It also has subsidiary currents, which do not touch the centre of the Church. For example, there is 'reverse mission' or the evangelising action that missionaries in the Third World can carry out in their mother churches. So a North American missionary in Africa can explain what he has done in the 'mission fields' to his colleagues, neighbours or friends. In the same way in the early Church the churches of the diaspora made a collection for the 'saints' in Jerusalem (2 Cor. 8-9), and so gave thanks for the gift of the Good News. But this is not what we are dealing with. We are talking about something more basic and more profound.

While it is true that the Gospel came from Israel, Israel nevertheless gave way to the Gentiles: 'They (my brothers of Israel) were adopted as sons, they were given the glory and the covenants . . . . Does this mean that God has failed to keep his promise? Of course not. Not all those who descend from Israel are Israel, not all the descendants of Abraham are his true children' (Rom. 9:4-7). And 'I will say to No-People-of-Mine, "You are my people" . . . . In the place where they were told, "You are no people of mine", they will be called "The sons of the living God"' (Hos. 2:23,3:1. Paul is quoting from him).

The tragedy of the 'rejection of Israel' has its logic. The Messiah was consecrated 'to bring the Good News to the poor' (Isa. 61:1; Luke 4:18). 'The good news is proclaimed to the poor' (Luke 7:22), and Jesus adds, 'and happy is the man who does not lose faith in me'. Why? Because from the moment the poor receive the good news, the *'centre' is shifted* and the 'power' of the Gospel is now not exercised from 'palaces'—be they in Jerusalem or Rome—but from the 'deserts' and by their 'prophets'.

And what actually happened was that Jerusalem began to receive challenges from the communities of the diaspora and to learn from them that salvation was for all, that the narrow nationalism of Jerusalem had to be overcome, that the Gospel was for all peoples and not just for the Jews: 'It makes no distinction between Jew and Greek: all belong to the same Lord who is rich enough, however many ask for his help' (Rom. 10:12).

In the same way, peripheral Ireland became a new missionary centre, with its influence flowing back to the 'continent' from which it received its faith, and evangelising it. Like Columba in the fifth century, so Winfrid (675-755), under the name of Boniface, became the apostle to the Germans. This is like the Gospel 'flowing' back again: from the pagans on to the shore of Israel, from Ireland on to the shores of the continent. We are beginning to see the *same process at work today*. After five centuries of evangelisation of the periphery, the periphery we now call the Third World, its poor are apparently 'flowing' back on to the mother churches to remind them of the *essence* of the

Gospel, which had become a little lost under triumphalism, riches, pride in being the first, the oldest, the wisest, the most 'devout', the most disciplined, the most ordered, the cleanest, the most civilised . . . .

From Russia and Poland to Europe and the United States, Catholics and Protestants are both beginning to be challenged by their brethren of the South, of the 'poor' Churches of Latin America, Africa and Asia. This 'flow' is not easy; it meets with resistance, closing of ears, defences, and, finally, 'control' of the message when a window has mistakenly been left open. *This secret, hidden, unarticulated opposition to the poor*—found equally in Rome or Constantinople or Moscow, not to mention Paris or New York—*is largely fear of losing control*: it is fear of universality, of what is new, like the fear the Judaizers of Jerusalem felt faced with the pagans to whom Paul had taken the Good News. But this 'flow' of the Gospel will become an irresistible flood tide, because the poor live the Gospel in a basic manner, as something 'natural' (what 'goes without saying', obviously, with no problems). The Gospel belongs to them, it is their property. The hopes of the Kingdom are the hopes of the poor for clothing, food, shelter, security, justice . . . 'their' God; because they are 'his people'. Now the 'saints' of the centre, if they want to be saints, must make common cause with the poor of Africa, of Asia, of Latin America, or with the 'Blacks' (Afro-American) and the 'Chicanos' (Latin-American) in the US, or with the 'guest workers' (from the poor countries of Southern Europe and North Africa) in Europe. When these poor people are Christian, the 'flow' we are talking about begins.

A purely *numerical* fact has been noted by Thomas Stransky, who writes: 'By the year 2000 from 55 to 60 per cent of all Christians (70 per cent of all Catholics) will be living outside North America and Europe'[6]; but the question is *qualitative*, as we shall see. This led Pius Wakatama to propose a 'moratorium'[7], which was initially merely a restriction: ' . . . rather, national leaders should be given responsibility and only a select number of *key* missionaries should be allowed to stay in direct teaching positions'.[8]

But, the *question is far more than one of numbers.* In *Asia*, Christianity, as in the early Church, is teaching how to be Christian in countries with a non-Christian majority, composed of other great religions (Hindu, Moslem, Buddhist). In *Africa*, Christians are showing how to take old non-Christian cultures into account in the liturgy, in order to re-define (re-invent) Christian celebration. In *Latin America*, Christians are showing how to take the option for the poor in the midst of their economic and political struggle for liberation. All these local churches are new (with the exception of those in Northern Africa or Ethiopia and Kerala in India), poor, needy . . . but full of the renewed strength of the Spirit. What they have learned from the Gospel—

despite the scandal of the expansion of European-Anglo saxon Christendom, as though through a miracle worked by God with his poor—about the *poor and crucified Christ* (who is opposed to the *rich and triumphally* civilised Christians of Europe and North America), they experience now in a paradigmatic fashion, and *witness this way of living their Christianity to the 'centre'.* The martyrdom of Mgr Oscar Romero in El Salvador, the heroic poverty of Mgr Pedro Casaldáliga in Brazil, the example of Bishop Desmond Tutu in South Africa, of the 'fishermen' in Kerala, of the Christians in the Philippines, are today 'universal' evangelising facts of undeniable 'spiritual' force, paradigmatic, missionary to the world of 'central' Christianity.

3. 'SOLIDARITY': THE NEW NAME FOR CATHOLICITY AND MISSION

The present missionary stage reached by Christianity is changing its meaning. We are at the end of the 'missionary age' and at the beginning of that of 'solidarity' (*koioía*: 2 Cor. 9:13) among 'local' churches. The centripetal North-South movement has changed into a circle: this encircles Christian life. Now Rome learns from Latin America, Geneva from Africa, New York from the Philippines or China. It is the *age of a new universality.*

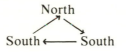

The 'circulation' of the Spirit is not only from South to North and vice-versa. It is equally from South to South. In Latin America in 1984, the Missions Department of CELAM, inspired among others by the missionary work of Marins and his team, which founds Basic Communities all over the world (I remember meeting Marins by pure chance in Tokyo airport in 1981; I was coming from the Philippines and he was going to India . . . and we talked all night about 'South-South' missions and our mutual responsiblity), produced the document *Ha llegado la hora* (*The time has come*): the 'time' for the church of Latin America (and Africa, and Asia) to state *its missionary responsiblities toward the other continents of the Third World* (South-South), and—why not?—toward the 'mother' churches (South-North).

Christian solidarity means the co-responsiblity that Christians exercise with regard to other 'local' churches (and the churches of Rome and Geneva are themselves 'local' in the unity of the same Spirit). Co-responsibility in liturgical, economic, ecclesial life in general. *A 'circular' co-responsibility of all for all.*[9] In this way we move from a model of *dominant uniformity* (bureaucratic Catholicism) to that of the pluriformity of the time of Vatican II, and beyond that to a *genuinely mutual* model, in which the pluralism of uncaring co-existence is taken up into the *co-responsible unity of universal solidarity* of a Church that is *one* not through the rule of *extrinsic* and authoritarian obedience (*imposed* unity), but through the organic structuring of mutual, co-responsible solidarity (unity from the *inner life* of the Spirit of Jesus and the Father)—'community' (*koinonía*).

When this happens, the churches of the 'centre' *open up* to the witness of the poor churches of the 'periphery'. They no longer seek to *control* their witness (as in the case of a missionary organisation which sees itself being unable to publish certain works originating in the periphery because they are too 'advanced', 'unsure' in their teaching, etc. Which means: the words of *criticism* and *protest* from the poor are controlled). This is the level on which we should seek to understand the recent confrontation between the Congregation for the Doctrine of the Faith and the Theology of Liberation from the periphery. The 'centre' is protecting itself fearfully from what the poor on the periphery are achieving (and in this sense the fine and ancient Slav church of Poland is just as much of the 'centre'). It feels challenged, humiliated, required to change . . . and it resists. It fails to see, however, that the *Christianity of the 'centre' is the product of an ambiguous identification with Mediterranean and European culture, and later with the capitalist system.* Both identifications are now 'prisons', straightjackets from which the Church must break free if it is to open out to a new universality (beyond Western culture and capitalism as a historically necessary system). It is at this stage of conversion in order to go beyond (the basic transcendentality of the Gospel) both limits—walls (Eph. 2:14-15)—that the poor who had been evangelised since the fifteenth century are becoming the evangelisers of the latter part of the twentieth century; 'But now in Christ Jesus, you that used to be so far apart from us have been brought very close, by the blood of Christ. For he is the peace between us . . . ' (Eph. 2:13).

4. THE PROPHETIC-EVANGELIZING CHURCH OF THE POOR

The 1980 Conference for World Mission and Evangelism in Melbourne began with a theme: 'The Good News to the poor' (Sec. 1).[10] I remember the first preparatory meeting when we were given the subject 'The Kingdom of God and the poor'[11]: 'God identified with the poor and oppressed by sending his Son Jesus to live and serve as a Galilean speaking directly to the common people'.[12] I also remember the time I spent working as a carpenter in Nazareth, from 1959-61. One day Billy Graham came to preach, in English, to the poor Christian Arab workers in the very town in which Jesus lived. What a surprise to hear the terms in which this Western 'missionary' preached the Gospel to those men and women! What sureness, pride, haughtiness even, this rich foreigner brought to his exposition of the Gospel to those poor people from Jesus' own country! Would it not have been more appropriate for this fundamentalist preacher to go down on his knees and ask those *poor* people to preach the Gospel to him? For me, working ten hours a day beside them, unable to communicate as I was learning modern Hebrew and spoke no Arabic, he seemed the prototype of the *missions* of the Christian West: aggressive domination over other peoples. This is why the point was made at Melbourne that, 'the concept of mission being from *sending* to *receiving* countries has long been replaced by a *mutuality in shared missions* involving a two-way flow between the churches in the industrialised countries and the so-called Third World' (IV, 23).[13] But there is more to it, as I have said before: the 'solidarity' (co-responsibility or mutuality) is practised first and foremost from a 'focus', from a 'nucleus', from a 'community' in which the Gospel flows most clearly, most prophetically, most deeply, most spiritually. This evangelising *locus par excellence* is the 'Church of the Poor', or *that part* of the Churches which is implanted among the 'objectively' poor: among the poor nations, the poor classes, the shanty town dwellers, minorities, tribes, ethnic groups, the 'wretched of the earth', in Franz Fanon's phrase.[14]

When a basic Christian community—let's take that in Riobamba, where Mgr Proaño was bishop till recently—meets; when those *poor people's hands*, calloused from hard daily work, split by the cold of the Andes, prematurely aged by exploitation . . . when those hands *take up the Bible*; when those eyes dimmed by malnutrition and disease *read the Bible*; when those mouths whose lips are split by thirst, and by the boss's blows, by the precariousness of their tenure . . . when those lips open *to explain the Gospel*; when those men and women, young people and children make up a *community*, all together sharing their goods with one another, breaking the eucharistic Bread on the tables where they knead the dough to make their daily bread and prepare their beans for their meagre meals, on which the mothers give birth to their children . . . who can these people be compared to? Is the basilica of St Peter's a more sublime place than the humble house of these Indians of the Andes?[15]

This 'Church of the poor', a component part of the one Church, but its most uncontaminated, most prophetic, most martyrial 'part', is what today is becoming *prophetically missionary and hope-bearingly evangelising*. This is the church that can convert, that can move the hearts of all young people, of all men and women of good will, in both the 'centre' and the 'periphery'. Now the evangelised poor are *becoming the evangelisers*:

> In the days to come—it is the Lord who speaks—
> I will pour out my spirit on all mankind.
> Your sons and daughters shall prophesy,
> your young men shall see visions,
> your old men shall dream dreams.
> Even on my slaves, men and women,
> in those days, I will pour out my spirit. (*Praxis* 2:17-18)

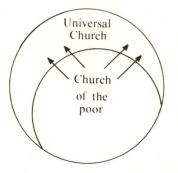

Gerald Anderson rightly wrote that at Melbourne 'the focus was on *the poor* in relation to the kingdom'[16], and so the final message declared that the poor would mean 'in many cases . . . a radical change in the institutional life of the missionary movement'.[17] More still, this presence of the poor 'as Church' in the churches (Catholic, Protestant or Orthodox) is a challenge to change not only in missionary institutes but in the *mother churches themselves* in their very life in the 'centre'. The churches of the 'centre' are defending themselves against this change. I remember the opposition of some members of the Roman Curia when Meetings of Third World Theologians were—and are— organised. A theology from the Third World, how can that be? Surely all theology is *one* and *universal?* There is then opposition to the voice of the poor reaching not only the 'centre' but the other churches of the 'periphery' as well. There is mistrust, fear, doubt . . . . In reality what they are *afraid of is losing identifications which tie the Church to the past: to Western culture, to capitalism, to power, to domination* . . . . It is a challenge of poverty, simplicity, hope. The 'spirit' of John XXIII, who had experienced a poor and oppressed 'periphery' in Turkey, teaches us to know how to learn from the other, the poor, the other 'local' churches.

Obviously, for the poor to 'evangelise' they must be listened to, must be seen as worthy bearers of the Gospel, as subjects of the Kingdom, as 'Jesus himself' in history amongst us. But for this to be possible, we have to leave our windows open. How could the Samaritan have seen the poor man who had been attacked and robbed if there had been a wall between him and the road? We have to knock down walls, or at least knock windows in them, if we are to see the poor. But we also need humility, poverty, openness . . . very difficult spiritual attitudes for the present world of the 'centre' to adopt.

Movements like 'Sanctuary' in the United States, in which Christians of the 'centre' open themselves to poor immigrants to their country from the periphery, receiving them even though this means breaking the existing laws against 'aliens' (particularly if they are poor and come from capitalist countries and so are no use for purposes of propaganda against socialist countries), enable these Christians to be evangelised by the poor and to become in their turn an evangelising 'church of the poor' in the midst of their 'centre' churches.[18] Such conversions to justice are the fruit of evangelisation, of the mission of the poor: they teach us how to live a more demanding, real, earthy, true Gospel.

In this way the 'flow' of the Gospel has begun, just begun. In the near future, as the crisis builds up, when the exploitation of the poor countries has become still more inhuman, when the conflict between capitalism and socialism has become irreversible, the Christian communities in the midst of the poor (poor countries, poor classes, poor groups of people, poor individuals) will become more and more exemplary, evangelising. They will suffer in their flesh the oppression of the poor and the same sufferings as Jesus underwent. They will evangelise.

Translated by Paul Burns

Notes

1. See O. Costas *Christ outside the Gate: Mission beyond Christendom* (New York 1982), biblio. pp. 195-227; D.S. Amalorpavadass *Approach, Meaning and Horizon of Evangelization* (Bangalore 1973); *The Theology of the Christian Mission* ed. G. Anderson (New York 1961); J.H. Bavinck *An Introduction to the Science of Missions* (Philadelphia 1960); A. Shorter *Theology of Mission* (Indiana 1972); O. Barres *World Mission Windows* (New York 1963); Choan-Seng Song *Christian Mission in Reconstruction: an Asian Analysis* (New York 1977); Leslie Newbigin *The Open Secret* (Grand Rapids 1978).
2. See D. Senior-Carroll Stuhlmueller *The Biblical Foundation for Mission* (New

York 1983); J. Power *Mission Theology Today* (New York 1971); C. Couturier *The Mission of the Church* (Baltimore 1959).

3. In Greek the title of the book of the *Acts* or *Deeds* of the Apostles is '*Praxis* of the Apostles'. I should like to refer to it under this most appropriate heading.

4. See my article 'The Expansion of Christendom, its Crisis and the Present Situation' in *Concilium* 144 (4/1981), pp. 44-50; Working Commission on Church History *Towards a History of the Church in the Third World* ed. L. Vischer (Berne 1985). *idem. Asia and Christianity* ed. M.D. David (Bombay 1985).

5. Sermon by Rev. Joseph Carey on 'The Philippines' in *The First American Catholic Missionary Congress* (Chicago 1909)—the Congress was held from 15-18 Nov. 1908. For the Protestant tradition see C. Forman 'A History of Foreign Mission Theory in America' in *American Missions in Bicentennial Perspective* (South Pasadena 1977) pp. 69-140 (biblio. pp. 115-40); C. Chanoy *The Birth of Missions in America* (South Pasadena 1976).

6. In 'Ecumenism from 1960 into the 1980's' in *Witnessing to the Kingdom, Melbourne and Beyond* (New York 1982) p. 68.

7. *Independence for the Third World Church. An African Perspective on Missionary Work* (New York 1978).

8. *Ibid.* p. 112. He also says: 'I question the sincerity of those who have no concern at all for the salvation of pagan American Blacks, Chicanos, Whites, Indians and others, but will cross oceans to reach and love these same people in other parts of the world' (p. 21). Missionaries should be sent only as 'teachers at high levels' (p. 112). See 2 Tim. 2:2.

9. See J. Sobrino & J. Hernández Pico *Theology of Christian Solidarity* (New York 1985).

10. *Witnessing to the Kingdom* pp. 105ff.

11. See *International Review of Mission* (Geneva 1980) pp. 115-30. I recall that my name caused objections on the part of the Roman Congregation responsible for ecumenism because of our commitment with reference to the Puebla Conference. We had to defend the 'poor' even against the position of some people in our mother Church.

12. *Witnessing* . . . , cited in note 6, Sec. I, 1, pp. 105-6.

13. *Ibid.* p. 164.

14. See my article' "Populus Dei" in populo pauperum: From Vatican II to Medellín and Puebla' in *Concilium* 176 (6/1984), pp. 35-44.

15. When I have been in Rome, I have always gone down to St Peter's catacomb (under the great basilica) and remembered in my prayers a little church by Lake Tiberias, near Capharnaum and the Mount of the Beatitudes (where I spent a time as a fisherman in the kibbutz of Guinosar), called 'the church of St Peter'. In that church, no more than twenty feet long, I think St Peter would have felt closer to his poor fishing community.

16. Introduction to *Witnessing* . . . , the work cited in note 6, p. 2.

17. *Ibid.*

18. The Board of Global Ministries of the United Methodist Church in the USA has initiated a praiseworthy programme in which ministers from the periphery (Latin America, Asia and Africa) preach to communities in the USA on the life of their poor churches (see *Like unto a Mustard Seed. The Struggle for Community*, Cincinnati 1985). But we need to go much further still.

Samuel Rayan

Irruption of the Poor: Challenges to Theology

INTRODUCTION

MOST 'THIRD World People' are *people of faith*. We have throughout our history sought to relate *our faith and our life* to each other, and to regrasp and remould the one in terms of the other. We wish to be no less contextual today. Today we find ourselves in a world of accelerating change, shrinking distances and mounting crisis. There is the crisis of values and of culture, crisis in economy and political life, crisis of environment and crisis caused by violence and repression. At the root of the malaise stands 'not resource scarcity or price rise or population pressure, but the world structure'.[1] The general context of the Third World is *global Capitalism, with its division of the world* and of most nations into the poor and the rich. For the masses of the Third World this structure spells death. The massive misery of the dispossessed of the earth, and the cry of the poor of the designedly underdeveloped periphery of Asia, Africa, Latin America and the South Pacific impel us to search in the realm of economies, politics and culture, as well as in our faith, scriptures and celebrations for resources with which we may *understand and overcome the structure of violence and wretchedness.*

Movements of the poor are part of the search. The poor who form the bulk of the world's population, are breaking out of the dark holes, the ghettoes, slums, Reservations and Bantustans, and the silence and self-contempt in which dominant classes have for centuries tried to consign us. We are breaking into the thick of history, into the halls of the Powerful, into élite fortresses where decisions are made which (mis)shape history and affect us, the poor, fatally. In one of Jesus' stories (Luke 16:19-31), the poor man

Lazarus, covered with sores and hungry, lay at the (nameless) rich man's gate. Today's Lazaruses will no longer lie at the gate and wait. We want to hear and heed the summons to 'stand erect, and hold your heads high, for your liberation is near' (Luke 21:28). We break the gate open and walk into the Great Eater's banquet hall and demand our share. This disturbs his comfort, his culture and his devotions. The irruption of the poor takes many forms. There is a general awakening and reaching out for freedom; there are the anti-colonial struggles; resistance in South Africa; wars of liberation in Vietnam, Mozambique, Nicaragua; there is the hope aroused by these events, and the part played both by religious faith and Marxist vision in kindling courage and sustaining the fight. There is the combat against racism, sexism, untouchability and classist organisation of society.

That means the process of liberation is happening within the very textures of oppression. This complex social reality of death, struggle and hope is led to interact with our faith. They question and interpret each other, and disclose new depths of challenge and meaning. Where Faith and social reality thus meet *theology sparks*: a theology which can uphold both the transcendental dimension of God's Reign and the New Person on the one hand and their historical and political dimensions on the other, without the reductionism to which Marxism and traditional theology have both succumbed.

Susan George advises us to '*study the rich and powerful not the poor and powerless . . . let the poor study themselves . . . .* If you truly want to help them, give them a clearer idea of how their oppressors are working'. Work done on organisation and resistance of the poor is avidly read by our enemies and used against us. We shall therefore reflect briefly on certain features of the enemy, the dominant system in which we live and against which we organise action.

1.   CONTEXT: CAPITALISM

(a) With the development of Capitalism into a world system, there is now *only one world market. The Capitalist one.* The Third World is an integral part of it, and the Socialist countries have been drawn into its vortex through investment and trade. So much so that Socialist countries not only participate enthusiastically in the Capitalist international division of labour under the laws and rules of the latter, but are affected by crises in Capitalist economy and are therefore anxious to prevent or solve such crises which once theoretically they had sought to sharpen unto capitalism's undoing.[2] There seems to be a high level of cultural penetration, too, of the Third World and

Socialist countries. The rich West defines goals, the rest pick up the model and talk of catching up. The West's technology then becomes a necessity, and no technology is culturally neutral.[3]

(b) Due to accumulation and competition the Capitalist system periodically runs into crisis, and *its centre shifts*. Since the fifteenth century the centre has shifted from North Italy to the Iberian States to England and to the U.S.A. The crisis manifests itself through decline in the rate of profit. To raise profits again, costs of production are reduced through far-reaching changes in the international Capitalist division of labour. The burden is shifted to the Third World today chiefly through the International Monetary Fund which imposes higher unemployment, lower wages, cut in welfare expenditure, production for export and devaluation of currency to make exports and foreign investment cheaper. To these economic measures correspond political policies of conservative governments and authoritarian tendencies in the West, and dictatorships, military governments and armed conflicts in the Third World.[4]

· (c) Capitalism as a world economic system has proved *a failure*. Its essential incapacity to satisfy humankind's basic needs—food, shelter, health, and community—has been palpably demonstrated. The experience of the poor masses of the Third World is more than proof. In India by official admission 317 million were below the poverty line in 1980 after over three decades of Capitalist development. The case of Brazil is most striking. Capitalist economists and politicians like M. Friedman and H. Kissinger praised Brazil's development as an 'economic miracle'. But the miracle was short lived: 1968 to 1973. The system broke down under weight of its inner contradictions and inequality. The whole development was limited to between 5% and 20% of the population. 20% took 62% of the national income; economic growth was structurally oriented to minority needs. The poor remained poor and became more miserable. Women and children were super-exploited. Workers toiled for 7 days a week for 12 to 16 hours a day for very low wages, with a very high accident rate. Thanks to massive influx of foreign capital and loans, Brazil's foreign debt rose from $4 billion in 1968 to 40/50 billion in 1979, which is 3 to 4 years' total export earnings; the service costs and interests eat up 2/3 of foreign exchange earnings.[5] ILO information for August 1985 points out that a vast majority of nearly one billion people caught in the poverty trap in developing countries eke out a precarious living in rural areas. Given Capitalist development, unemployment and poverty are likely to accelerate in the Third World, together with an increase in pollution and depletion of nature and in the possibility of armed conflict.[6]

The system breeds poverty in the rich countries too. The U.S. Bureau of

Census, 1972, admits that 'at least 10 to 12 million Americans are starving or sick because they have too little to spend on food'. By 1975, the number of the poor in the U.S. grew by 2.5 million; 12.3 percent of the population now lives in poverty.[7] The film *Mother Teresa* by Ann and Jeannette Petrie, screened in the U.N. General Assembly Hall on October 26, 1985 began with shots of Calcutta, but soon enough it turned to sights of poverty elsewhere: a man in rags on a busy street in the heart of New York searching for eatables in a garbage heap. People are discovering an America they had never known existed: an America of the hungry, the homeless, the uncared for and the forlorn. Andrew H. Malcolm writing in the *N. Y. Times* describes 'a vast new class of poor Americans' and claims that 'about 13.8 million Americans under the age of 18, and 48% of all black children live in poverty'. The president of German Caritas, writing in the organisations magazine has noted that in West Germany poverty is on the increase. The growth of poverty in the richest capitalist countries is a telling comment on the nature of this dominant economic system.

Another comment would be the way Capitalism ensnares Third World countries in a *vicious debt trap*. Third World debt has multiplied. The greatest debts have been run up by countries who have followed I.M.F. policies and participated actively in export promotion and international division of labour. The indebtedness of Latin American countries, for instance, has reached an incredible 360 billion, requiring about $40 billion in amortisation and interest payment annually. Millions of workers have had their wages cut, and millions have been laid off. The 'debt morass' persists. Debtors have no money left over for production investment after they make their loan payments. In them have appeared authoritarian governments and military regimes using severe repression to silence protest and dissent. There seems to be a correlation between economic difficulties and political repression. C. Payer has pointed out that the list of countries under attack for human rights violation is nearly identical with the list of those with imminent debt problems.[8]

From a survey of unequal accumulation in seven Third World countries, A.G. Frank concludes that 'in none of these economies is there any prospect that the masses of the population will in the foreseeable future, share the benefits of this growth model to any substantial extent'.[9] The Capitalist development solution 'has brought nothing but misery to the poor and new dependence while enriching the already rich world'.[10]

Capitalism, then, is a badly organised socio-economic system. It is of little use for human purposes. Even after the last five hundred years of 'economic growth', basic human needs remain far from satisfied for the majority. The reason is not that we have not worked and produced. The reason is that 'production has been organised in the wrong way'.[11] *Capitalism is the wrong way.*

(d) It is not only a wrong way but *a violent and criminal way.* The failure to satisfy basic human needs is avoidable. The technical and social possibility of satisfying them exists. If then, they are not actually satisfied for so long, it means 'that there is violence at work'.[12] J.K. Galbraith illustrates the violence that assisted at the birth of modern capitalism. Tenants were expelled with fire and dogs. Houses were burned without evacuating the aged and the enfeebled. The use of women and children to work thirteen hours a day in the mills. The loot and larceny connected with the American railroad. 'The casualty rates of those who ran the trains—the incidence of mutilation and death—approached that of a first class war.' Trade and profit were protected by the British Government while famine, starvation and death raged in Ireland, 1845-1847.[13] One could recall the cruelty of merchant Capitalism's wars, conquests, colonial rule, plunder, genocidal policies, slave trade, destruction of economies and cultures and other mechanisms of inducing underdevelopment. The violence of Capitalist practice was philosophically underpinned by Herbert Spencer, social Darwinist, for whom to help the poor was to interfere with the improvement of the race. The poor were to be used and sacrificed for the development of the rich.[14]

Violence, then, is in the nature and logic of the system. 'Bourgeois (capitalist) thinking entails an unlimited justification of violence. There is no atrocity that cannot be commited in the name of this entrepreneurial metaphysics.' John Locke prescribes torture, slavery and death for the opponents of bourgeois society.[15] Torture, slavery and death precisely are what Capitalism's critics have been getting in most countries of Latin America, East and South Asia and Southern Africa; and in subtler ways in the South Asian region, and in the developed countries too. Capitalism means death not only to its opponents, but to the masses it exploits. 'The ownership of the means of production is at the same time the ownership of the means of subsistence, a question of life and death for those who sell their labour.' The inequalities which Capitalism creates and deepens 'are extremely lethal for those at the bottom' of the social pyramid.[16]

Even food is used as a means of domination and death. 'Food is a weapon . . . one of the principal tools of our negotiating kit', declared a U.S. Secretary of Agriculture. A.G. Frank cites other official voices to the same tune from the headquarters of World Capitalism.[17] Frank and Susan George show how, meanwhile, Third World agriculture is manipulated and distorted, and the Third World People are made to depend for food on the First World.[18]

Food is weapon. Food scarcity is often planned by not growing food, by withholding stocks from the market, by raising prices. The goal of the Third World élites and their Western supporters is not and never was 'to feed today's undernourished or starving millions, but to perpetuate poverty and dependence' for political and economic reasons.[19]

As a result forty or more million people die of hunger every year. In Brazil 86 million people are hungry, two thirds of them do not have a meal a day and 300 out of every 1000 children die before they are three months old. Yet Brazil 'could be the banquet table for the hungry of the whole world', that is, within a different system of production and distribution.[21]

2. CHALLENGE TO THEOLOGY

(a) Challenge to theology comes, in the first place, from *the death of the poor* within the coils of Capitalism and from the claims of life as represented by the resistance of the oppressed. Any theology which does not take these realities into account and does not in fact originate in them is at best irrelevant. The God of its discourse is likely to have the face or facelessness of capitalism. The resistance of the poor to capitalism implies a rejection of the God of King Uzziah and the Gods of all the kings, presidents and generals (Isa. 6:1-10).

The poor resist and refuse to acquiesce in misery and death. Their resistance implies an affirmation of realities other and deeper than death. The theological task is to join the resistance and from within it respectfully to explore the deeper significance of the centuries-old struggles of the oppressed against death and for life. *At the heart of the struggle, a vision of the future is unfolding*, a dream of some utopia. It is theology's task to clarify this dream and help move in the direction of its realisation. The long resistance of the people has fashioned a world of faith—faith in life and its promise. It is in this world of faith that the task of theology lies. It is there that the true God can emerge and be met. The true God is the living God. The living God is one who fosters life and sides with those who struggle for food, freedom, dignity and community against all systems of death and subjugation.

Biblical faith shaped up as a struggle of Hebrew slaves against oppression and death. That faith is inseparable from their opposition to oppression. Not that we first have faith, and in its light take the side of life. Rather, faith is the very act of siding with life. Are those, then, who are commited to capitalist economics and politics surrendering to a god of death in an inverse faith? Perhaps. Commitment to life and to struggle against systems of death is now as always the norm and measure of faith in the living God. Our theological task then, is to get closer to the reality of people burning yet refusing to be charred and immobilised: and to support every combat against death in all its varied forms, and foster the forces of life, freedom and hope. The task is to join in the ongoing struggles of the poor and discern there the seeds and stirrings of life in which the Earth's future lies, and in which God comes alive in history.

An awareness of death as the enemy and a quest for means to overcome it is central to *India's spiritual traditions*. An important myth tells of a joint endeavour by gods and humans, (half-brothers, all mortal) to churn the divine ocean of milk in which, they had learned, the Elixir of immortal life lay hidden. The ocean tried to deflect them by yielding many a tempting gift, but the quest continued till finally the precious elixir was in their hands. But then the gods practised deceit, stole the pot, drank from it and became immortal, leaving humans in the realm of death. The human struggle against exploitation and treachery continues, and within it the human quest for life in its fulness. At one point in this enterprise it was discovered that Siva (the Auspicious) was not just one of the gods, but *the* God of life who alone could tackle and subdue Cosmic Death by 'swallowing' it as it emerged from the ocean in the shape of a lump of poison which, if cast on the earth, would burn it to a heap of ashes in an instant. Siva, the source of life and joy symbolised by the Phallus, and encountered within the struggle against death, resembles the poor in his life-style and disdains ruling class manners and pieties. These are *stories of the people* with roots in forgotten socio-political experiences and operative still in the subconscious of the masses. If theology means to explore the depths and mobilise for the future, it cannot ignore such memories except at the risk of sacrificing effectiveness.

Jesus identifies as profoundly religious whatever is done for the furtherance of life (Matt. 25:31-40). Or, rather, he relates life more directly to God than he does conventional religion. Religious laws and practices are made to yield to human needs and celebration of life (Mark 2:15-28; 7:1-13). Life is for Jesus more profoundly 'religious' than religion itself. Here theology stands challenged to transcend its ecclesiastical-denominational confines, and concern itself with life in all its richness and with the mystery which is unfolding within life's vicissitudes.

· (b) Challenge to theology comes also from the fact that *Capitalism dehumanises* all who get caught in its claws: the rich no less than the poor. A system in which it is normal and necessary to plan food as weapon, to contrive famines, create unemployment, escalate the arms race, promote wars, put profit above people, use child labour, organise starvation wages, torture workers to discipline them, treat labour power and women as a (cheap) commodity, support dictators who rule by assassination, and kill multitudes through pollution—such a system is essentially brutalising. It drains all who are within its range of finer feelings and basic human values, unless they revolt and strive against it. No wonder Jesus and early Christians condemned accumulated wealth without qualification. (Luke 6: 24). The wealthy get dehumanised and dehumanise others. The story of the Great Eater illustrates the point (Luke 16:19-31). And the story of the Fool, too. (Luke 12:13-21). They became more thing than person. Jesus saw that accumulated and unshared wealth camelises people. (Mark 10:17-27).

Faith reflection has to dwell much more than it has so far done on the *Bible's criticism of wealth and power*, on Jesus' attitude to riches, and especially on what capitalism has done and is doing to people. Individualism not only blocks aspects of human blossoming, possible only in an equal and friendly social set-up; it invades the faith and contracepts the communitarian demands, for instance, of the practice of the Eucharist. The distortions in religious faith and human practice brought about by the invasion of Capitalism remain to be explored. Those who view the human as the crown of Creation/Evolution, and as the subject of history cannot accept the reduction of women and men to commodity status: still less can we, who see the Human as called to become the Image and Presence of God on this earth, and the place where God comes to be on Earth to realise the Self.

We agree with Howard Zinn's remark that no wars (which cost millions of lives) bring any gain for humanity that would be worth one human life.[21] Here is a theological judgment on capitalism's wars. Zinn can make it because he is reading history from the view point of its victims. But as the victims themselves become aware of the corrosive nature of the system and begin to resist it, they are also on the way to rebuilding their pride and winning back their humanity. That is a 'theological' process; it keeps pace with the process of the coming of the Kingdom and with the formation in the womb of history of the Human in which alone God can emerge and dwell among us in an exchange of Grace.

(c) Theology stands challenged, thirdly, by *the idolatrous character of Capitalism.* Once bourgeois society was atheistic. That was during its struggle for political power against feudalism of which Religion was an ally. Then as socialism came to birth in opposition to Capitalism but at one with it in its materialist stance and its rejection of transcendence, Capitalism panicked. The returns of anti-socialist propaganda for profit would not be large if the two antagonistic systems had common grounds in atheism. Capitalism therefore began to wear the mantle of religion once worn by Feudalism which by now was dead or dying. Today it is scared of atheism. It sees in atheism a challenge to the various forms of domination it seeks to impose on the peoples of the world.[22] In religion on the other hand it sees a tool which can be subtly used to persuade people to maintain the status quo, to respect the market, to stand in awe of political power and its law and order, to reverence commodities and be devoted to consumerism. Capitalism today talks the language of religion, supports individualistic other-wordly non-political theologies and spiritualities, which cannot rock the capitalist boat, and launches virulent attacks on theological and pastoral movements which defend the rights of the poor. South Africa's Botha claims Apartheid is 'a struggle of the Christian Western civilisation against the powers of darkness and Marxism'.[23] Latin American dictators and their U.S. patrons are protecting Christianity when they defend Capitalism by large scale repression and massacre. Rios Montt, Guatemala's military dictator 'preaches' every Sunday insisting he came to power 'by the direct instructions of God himself'.[24]

But the god of capitalism is not the Yahweh of Exodus; it will have nothing to do with liberation of the oppressed. It is not the Lord of Mary's Magnificat; its plan is to make the hungry hungrier. Nor is it represented by Jesus of the beatitudes and of social reversals (Matt. 20:16; Luke 9:48; 14:7-14). The object of Capitalism's cult is commodity and profit; it is money, private property, market laws, political power, individualism, competition and unhindered economic growth with no regard to what the System does to people.[25] In capitalism these are given an absolute character. The system has come to be called the American way of life. It is what the U.S. is pledged to defend 'regardless of the cost, and regardless of the peril'.[26] It is what the U.S. Embassy in the film *Missing* defends by collaborating in total massacre in Chile, 1973. A God, a theology, is implicit in all human practice. Oppressive practice implies the crucifixion of the true God in God's children, along with the worship of false gods. Liberative struggle implies the rejection of oppressor gods, and the celebration of the living God who liberates. The practice of Capitalism shows it resembles Moloch. It is Mammon, the only rival to the God of Jesus. Mammon is the body of greed. Greed 'is the same thing as worship of a false God' (Col. 3:5; and see Eph 5:5). Capitalism is armed and organised greed. Its history bears out this definition. When it spread over the earth idolatry spread. When it destroyed men and women, it destroyed the only living image of God on this earth.

The true God on the contrary sees the affliction of the people and joins the struggle of the oppressed themselves. The true God is one whose thoughts are with the people and the poor even when magnificient liturgies engulf him (Isa. 6:1-9). The idol, on the other hand, has no eyes for the wounds of the people, no ears for their cry. It has eyes for profit and power, and its heart conceives food as weapon (see Ps. 115).

In such a situation to speak a word about God is to denounce the system and deny its gods. Paradoxically theology must begin with atheism. With the early Christians we hold that the emperor is not God, nor is money, nor is capitalism nor any political order. We begin by denying the gods of the multinationals and generals who oppress and kill. We reject as the prophets rejected all worship divorced from justice and from struggles for the dignity and rights of the least of us. Without some form of atheism, with full affirmation of all the gods no faith in the true God is possible. The yardstick by which the gods are judged is justice; all the gods which connive at injustice shall die (Ps. 82). The space created by the removal of our oppressor's gods will be discovered as made possible and as inhabited by the God of justice and liberation. Our struggle brings us into the presence of the true God whom we tell out in story and song and the celebration of one another.

But to deny the gods of the emperor and the oppressor is to go political; as profoundly and dangerously political as the book of Revelation. To be non-political is to agree never to say in anyone's hearing that the emperor is not God and that capitalism is not absolute. To be non-political is to let the false gods rule, is to subscribe to idolatry. We have to name the Beast and refuse to identify the true God with oppressive power. God dwells not in power but 'in the faith, life and death of the poor.'[27] In history God appears in the 'flesh', in the weak and powerless classes, provoking them to say No to the armed might of money. Resistance to oppressive power is the pledge of God's friendly presence. The irruption of the poor into history calls for a theological assessment of the world of power. It asks if the conception of a dominator God has not given birth to dominator human beings, and to idolatry.

But, as we have seen, to resist the Beast is to risk life. Our theology means to equip us for martyrdom and for courageous witness to the possibility and necessity of a different set-up for the world. The objection to Capitalism is that in forging an unequal and, therefore, unfree society, it builds into the economic and political fabric of life a structural situation of idolatry. In projecting a different social vision, the organised dissent and witness-unto-death of the poor are outlining an understanding of God who can only be represented by a free community of equals.

With us our theology too must be prepared for martyrdom. A clear word about God who cannot be identified with socio-economic, military, ecclesiastical or political power will be rejected by those in power. A theology of the living God will not be acceptable to traders in a system that thrives through the death of people. Neither the message about a God who liberates nor the word about a God who dwells in peoples' struggles for dignity and freedom can be welcome news to Pharaohs, Herods and Caesars, old or new. Attempts will be made to silence prophetic theology; attempts such as Amos knew and Jeremiah too (Amos 7:12-13; Jer: 11:21-22). To the powerful who impose it, silence may be a problem. To the poor, the silencing of their theology is a symbol of the larger reality of the silencing of their culture and their history. To our theologians imposed silence is a fresh baptism into the crucified culture of the people. To all of us it is a place where the silence of God and of Jesus becomes history and confronts injustice (Mic. 3:4-7; Luke 23:9; Mark 15:5). Silence is a challenge to theology as well as a way of doing it.

This is the challenge: as the oppressed Son of Man, clad in silence and bound with chains, stands before King Herod, his whole Body calls out and says to us, the poor: 'Stand erect, hold your heads high, your liberation is near.'

Notes

1. J. Galtung *The True Worlds* (New York 1980) pp. 1-3.
2. A.G. Frank *Crisis: in the World Economy* (London 1980) pp. 178, 246-262, 315-321; and see *idem Crisis: In the Third World* (London 1981) pp. xi, xii.
3. See the work cited in note 1, at p. 109.
4. A.G. Frank *Crisis: In the World Economy* cited in note 2 at pp. 306-314; *idem Crisis: In the Third World* cited in note 2 at pp. xii-xiii, 82-83; J.R. Wogaman *The Great Economic Debate. An Ethical Analysis* (Philadelphia 1977) at p. viii.
5. A.G. Frank *Crisis: In the Third World* cited in note 2 at pp. 6-13.
6. See the work cited in note 1 at pp. 18-19.
7. S. George *How the Other Half Dies. The Real Reasons for World Hunger* (New York 1977) at pp. 30-31, 350.
8. A.G. Frank *Crisis: In the Third World* cited in note 2 at pp. 9, 11, 132, 153).
9. *Ibid.* pp. 61, 154.
10. See S. George the work cited in note 7 at p. 17.
11. J. Galtung the work cited in note 1 at pp. 21, 19.
12. *Ibid.* p. 21.
13. J.K. Galbraith *The Age of Uncertainty. A History of Economic Ideas and their Consequences* (Boston 1977) at pp. 27-30, 37-40, 49-53.
14. *Ibid.* pp. 45-48.
15. P. Richard *et al. The Idols of Death and the God of Life. A Theology* (New York 1983) pp. 167-168.
16. The work cited in note 1 at pp. 110, 112.
17. *Crisis: In the Third World* pp. 62-63.
18. *Ibid.* pp. 64-71, 76, 87-95; and see S. George the work cited in note 7 chapters 5, 7 and 8.
19. See S. George the work cited in note 7 at pp. 46, 139-157, 271, 19; and see Richard *et al.* the work cited in note 15 at pp. 179-181.
20. *Christian Worker* (Colombo) 3rd Q (1985) 43.
21. H.S. Zinn *A People's History of the United States* (New York 1980) p. 350.

22. See P. Richard *et al.* the work cited in note 15 at pp. 3-5.

23. See A.G. Frank *Crisis: In the Third World* cited in note 2 at p. 59; and see *Christian Worker* (Colombo) 2nd Q (1985) 43.

24. LADOC (Latin American Documentation) XIV No.1 (Sept./Oct.) 1983.

25. J.K. Galbraith the work cited in note 13 at pp. 82-83; and see P. Richard *et al.* the work cited in note 15 at pp. 171-172, 189-192.

26. F. Greene *The Enemy. Notes on Imperialism and Revolution* (Calcutta 1971) p. 17.

27. P. Richard *et al.* the work cited in note 15 at p. 151.

Walter Fernandes

The Challenge of Catholic Education

AFTER TWO development decades most social analysts have come to realise that the present pattern of development has in fact led to the *widening of the gap between rich and poor countries and within the Third World itself* between the élite and the masses. This stratification and impoverishment are as evident in education as in other sectors. For a Third World theology to be relevant, it is important to understand the situation that has led to these inequalities. We shall, therefore, at first study the main aspects of *stratification* in the Third World (particularly India), see its expression in the educational system and then go on to reflect on the role of Christians in this situation.

1. THE SITUATION OF INEQUALITIES

A striking feature of most Third World societies is their hierarchical structure, in every field. Those who are on the lowest rank (known in India as the Scheduled Castes) are economically, socially, politically and culturally marginalised i.e. are victims of 'cumulative inequalities'. This stratification can be seen in the ownership of assets and division of income, health status, literacy etc. In India in 1972 the bottom 20% owned less than 2% of its assets while the top 5% owned nearly 50%. Also malnutrition, poor health, high mortality particularly among children (40% of whom are malnourished) are primarily among the assetless rural poor, most of whom are landless, belong to the low castes and live below the poverty line i.e. cannot afford 2250 calories per day.[1] These aspects are also closely linked to illiteracy, particularly among women.[2]

(a) Literacy Rates

Literacy rates themselves are linked to the caste, class, sex and urban-rural difference of the families. In India, for example, the literacy rate which was over 80% among urban upper class males in 1981, went down according to the class, caste, and sex of the people till it became 27.9% among rural Scheduled Caste males and 8.45% among their women.[3]

Briefly, *literacy symbolises inequalities* that exist in a society as a whole. The bottom 20% of Indian Society who own less than 2% and live below the poverty line do not have access to education and other services. On the other hand, monopoly over education ensures that those who have access to élite schools also monopolise the high status jobs as many studies of the caste and class origin of medical doctors, engineers and other high status professions have shown.[4] In other words, education serves as the most important *reproductive system of society*.

(b) The Historical Context

Studies on the origin of the educational institutions in Third World countries which were former colonies of European nations have shown that the colonial society was essentially a *three tier system* made up of (i) the ruling race on top, (ii) the upper class local population in the middle and (iii) the other local population at the bottom. Colonialism was in practice a mode of a foreign country ruling the local population through the collaboration of the upper classes of that country. Education had to play its role of transmitting the colonial cultural heritage to ensure the reproduction of this stratification. The very first British policy-document on education in India stated that its purpose was to remove power from the dominant classes, integrate them into the British system through the colonial language i.e. English and turn them into collaborators of the coloniser. These dominant classes would then pass British commercial values on to the other groups, make Western dress and products respectable and thus create a market for British textiles and other industrial products, which were needed if the colony was to be exploited for economic purposes.[5] This was legitimised in the name of 'civilising education'. While removing legal inequalities based on caste and sex, the educational system that catered to the upper class standards and timings and was arranged to suit British colonial needs, ensured that it became inaccessible to those who could not 'come up to these standards' or needed their children at home during the day to supplement the meagre income of their parents.[6]

The net result was that the rich who were already strong and had socio-economic power, enhanced it further by adding to it English education and professional status. It is these classes that took control of the Freedom Movement and in 1947 the British transferred political power to them. These groups with a vested interest in the *status quo* have ensured that all development is geared to the needs of their class.

Coming to education, while universal primary education is the declared policy of the government, investment in primary education has decreased from 55% of the total outlay for education during the first five year plan (1951-1956) to 35.9% in the sixth (1980-85).[7] Allotment to higher education has increased. Briefly, the structure needed for the powerful has been further strengthened at the cost of the powerless. We have seen its consequences in the form of malnutrition, infant mortality, illiteracy and greater marginalisation among the weaker sections.

2.   CHRISTIAN EDUCATION

The origin of Catholic schools has to be situated within this colonial context. The missionary was convinced that education imparted through the English medium was the most fruitful means for the *conversion of Indians to Christianity* and that once the upper classes saw their superstition and were converted, Christian knowledge would filter down to the other classes.[8] Soon, however, social reality would catch up with the missionaries. The schools were catering to the upper class aspirations of social promotion in the colonial system without leading to any conversion. A new legitimation of 'Praeparatio evangelica' was found in the belief that the schools functioned as a long-term preparation for the filtration of Christian values.[9] Eventually, however, even this argument would not be very convincing, since very few conversions followed after several decades. Finally, 'Christian influence in the administration in a British Protestant dominated country' became the sole justification. In their desire to 'save souls', without their realising it, the missionary schools only prepared upper class administrators and filtration agents of British cultural and commercial values, and in the process re-inforced the local and colonial dominant classes' hold over the poorest sections.

The trend of catering to the upper classes has continued also after Independence. The number of university colleges run by Catholics has grown by 500 per cent and high schools by more than 100 per cent while primary schools have gone up by only 15 per cent.[10] Evangelisation and the security of the Christian community was declared the main motive for this. Catholic leaders perceived their own society as a minority in a Hindu-dominated India. The leaders concluded that in such a situation Christians had to find security first of all by building institutions that would strengthen the middle class in their own community and simultaneously by opening more English medium schools for the children of the upper class decision-makers in order to have influence among the powerful groups for the security of the Church.[11]

After independence there have been several attacks against Christians but they have been mostly in feudal states where Christians are primarily tribals or are of low caste origin. The feudal elements view conversion as a first step to the liberation of those whom they have kept under their control for centuries, and oppose their conversion for fear that they would be educated and would be free from their bondage. However, because of a lack of analysis of the *socio-economic forces at work*, Christian leaders view this as a purely religious problem and keep building institutions to cater to the upper classes with the hope of getting their co-operation in evangelisation.

3.   THE CHALLENGE FOR CHRISTIANS

It is in the context of this *interaction of dominant forces and the evangelical motives of the Church* that the Christian challenge should be viewed. The Christian leaders looked at education as a tool for evangelisation or for the security of the Church. They did it without analysing the forces at work in the society at large. The dominant forces of this society have used these inputs for their own advancement, without in any way supporting the weaker sections. In other words, in India, as in most Third World countries, the Church has got involved in an important social reproductive system like education for a purely religious motive of the security of the Church without analysing the forces at work. Consequently, even while hoping to serve the poor, *the Church has strengthened the already strong often at the cost of the poor*. Thus in order to safeguard its own interests, the Church has ended up by going against the mission of continuing the work of Him who became a slave in order to free the world from injustice and oppression.

And yet, *socio-economic inequality is a major challenge in the Third World*. It is reflected in education as in the rest of life. If properly directed, education can become a mode of social mobility for many marginalised groups. To achieve this, the churches in the Third World would have to rethink the meaning of the 'good of the Church' and would have to ask themselves whether they choose *to maintain the status quo* by searching for security with the powerful, *or become people of God* listening to the 'signs of the times'

(L.G. No.4). They would have to find legitimacy not in 'the good of the Church' but by responding to the social reality of glaring inequalities and denial of human rights to a large majority. These churches will have to realise that unless a *conscious choice is made to support the marginalised groups*, all their inputs will in fact interact with the forces at work in the society at large and, without the Church being conscious of it, continue to strengthen the already powerful.

Catholic education in the Third World can become relevant only if it is turned into a tool for the liberation of the powerless majority. As already mentioned, the present education responds to the value system and the culture of the powerful minority. The standards that result from this value system are imposed on the powerless majority who are unable to 'come up' to these standards. For education to become relevant to this marginalised majority, one has to begin by *respecting their culture and rethinking the very concepts of standards and quality.* Its methodology would have to reverse these attitudes, revalorise the 'culture of silence', and treat the powerless as persons capable of deciding for themselves and as groups with human rights, in this case the right to education. This education would have to create in the marginalised groups a sense of self-respect, facilitate a climate of action for liberation and bring out the creativity of groups that are considered uncivilised, but have been able to survive for centuries despite odds against them.

If this approach is accepted, then the *educational institutions will have to be re-oriented to suit the needs of the poor.* Priority will have to be given to universalisation of elementary education rather than higher level and university education. New non-formal methods will have to be attempted and the curriculum, timings and approach changed to suit the needs of the poor. Experience in countries like Nicaragua has shown that such a goal is attainable if the approach is changed.[12]

In this context the churches in the Third World will have to rethink the meaning of the 'security of the Church'. The temptation would be to find security with the few powerful. But if education has to be geared to the needs of the poor, then the churches in these countries will have to free themselves from this sense of security and face the reality of the insecure world of the marginalised groups, take risks and experiment with new approaches. Christian motivation will certainly be important for this risk-taking. The inspiration for this experimentation will come from Christ who took risks in His life—who died in order to give life. But this inspiration has to be guided by the social reality of inequalities if the Church is not to play into the hands of the already powerful. Thus more than in the rich countries, the Third World churches have to become open communities—open to the signs of the times, to the situation around them. In a spirit of faith, these churches have to make an option between security with the powerful with the acceptance of their value system, and experimentation and risk-taking to build communities of the poor and oppressed. *The liberating mission of Christ will have to be understood in the socio-economic context of these countries.*

CONCLUSION

We have examined in this paper, the socio-economic situation of a few countries of the Third World and have seen how the system of education in these countries has reproduced the stratification of their societies. It is in this context that the Churches in the Third World would have to make a choice. What does 'death on the cross in order to lead to resurrection' mean in these countries? When a large percentage of the people in these countries can only look forward to a life of death and despair, what does Christian hope mean in these societies? The liberation brought to the world by Christ has to be real to those who are oppressed.

It is from this point of view that education has to be examined and alternatives to the present system found. These alternatives would not be in the form of a few palliatives given to the poor but in changing the very system that keeps them oppressed. The system of education has to be made accessible by changing it in such a way that it caters to their needs. To achieve this, the Christian communities in these countries would have to re-examine the concept of security with the powerful in order to ensure the survival of the weak. This is the challenge of Catholic Education.

Notes

1. ILO, *Profiles of Rural Poverty* (Geneva: International Labour Organisation, 1979) pp. 14-15.

2. Meera Chatterjee 'Health for All: Whither the Child?' *Social Action* 35 (3) (1985) 225-228

3. Walter Fernandes 'Development and People's Participation: An Introduction in *Development with People: Experiments with Participation and Non-Formal Education* ed. Walter Fernandes (New Delhi: Indian Social Institute 1985) pp. 3-5

4. Imrana Qadeer 'Health Services in India: An Expression of Socio-economic Inequalities' *Social Action* 36 (3) (1986) 205-207.

5. B.B. Misra *The Indian Middle Classes: Their Growth in Modern Times* (London 1961) pp. 149-152.

6. J.P. Naik *Equality, Quality and Quantity: The Elusive Triangle of Indian Education* (New Delhi 1975) pp. 7-9.

7. C.M. Padmanabhan 'Resource Constraints for Indian Education' *Social Action* 36 (1) (1986) 42-53.

8. Melvyn J. Laird *Missionaries and Education in Bengal 1793-1837* (Oxford 1972) pp. 20-21.

9. G.A. Oddie *Social Movements in India: British Protestant Missionaries and Social Reforms, 1850-1900* (New Delhi 1978) pp. 22-23.

10. Walter Fernandes *The Indian Catholic Community: Its Peoples and Institutions in Interaction with the Indian Situation Today* (Brussels 1980) pp. 3-5.

11. Thomas Pothacamury *The Church in Independent India* (Bombay 1961) p. 110.

12. Robert F. Arnove *Education and Revolution in Nicaragua* (New Delhi 1983).

Richard A. Couch

Churches in Developed Countries and the People of the Third World

1. SOME PARTICULAR FACES

THE STRIKING differences between the developed and the Third world become especially clear as I write this, for *I am travelling somewhat extensively in Peru and Central America*, together with my wife and son, Twenty-seven years in seminary teaching and other ecumenical activities in Argentina and Uruguay have made the whole problematic of the Third world vs. the developed world amply clear but the human face of our experiences along the way this time has been particularly poignant. This took the form of two young Quechua Indian brothers, who, alone and smiling, welcomed us out of the driving rain into their mud-hut along the Royal Inca Trail on the way over the Andes Machu Picchu ruins. As we rearranged our packs and dried some clothing near the meagre fire in the corner, the older boy's eyes became large with envy as he leafed through our guide book. Though the book was in English he was fascinated with what he imagined it to be saying and disappointed because his parents now labouring in the valley—to return at an unspecified time—had determined that he would leave school and return to care for the hut-home.

The tale could go on at length. But *just evoking the different human faces*: the amazingly agile Quechua porters who navigated up and down the Inca Trail with all kinds of heavy luxury items so that wealthy developed-world trekkers would miss few of the comforts of home: young and committed government officials in Managua explaining cogently the course of the changes in Nicaragua, their deep concern for the welfare of the Nicaraguan people in the midst of disastrous odds and anxiety lest Washington begin to believe its own

120

rhetoric and initiate the threatened invasion; the rural cooperative near Matagalpa (Nicaragua) where fifty men, women and children—initially reticent, later jubilantly affectionate—showed us their homes and fields with great pride; valiant and clean country people with only the most minimal signs of prosperity—and a crude trenchwork to protect them from night incursions by the Contras; a small band of leather-faced indigenous women and one man 30 miles from the Honduran border, who are midwives and have received simple equipment and valuable training to upgrade their effectiveness but who with a certain frustrating frequency are unable to reach a woman giving birth because of the night activity of the Contras.

These quick views of some aspects of life in one corner of the Third World have, probably, their value as folklore. But the question that they pose goes far beyond folklore into world politics, world peace and the future of the race. Our current trip will take us now into Cuba and then, laden with all these encounters and sensitivities, we are to spend a month in New York and Philadelphia undertaking to communicate something humanly significant to Church groups and others.

The question is whether people's consciousness there allows them to *take into account the human and the Gospel meaning of all this poverty, suffering and postponement* in any more than a superficial sense—with all good intentions. In the first instance our answer can only be negative. In any case that is the kind of an answer that history has given. The ties between sensitive and caring peoples around the world—Christian or not—may have been significant in one way or another from time to time through the ages but the cruel wheels of history have rolled on over weaker peoples; never—or hardly ever—detained by the sensitivity of one people toward another or the power of ethical convictions to alter the reality of power and greed.

Perhaps then the only sensible approach to this *cross-cultural dimension of the ecclesiastical enterprise* is to curtail it or abandon it. But the question which we seek to ask and perhaps answer here is: within the resources of the world Christian community is there anything meaningful and effective which can happen, or be made to happen, which can have any significant impact on the way in which today's rich and powerful oppress today's poor and weak?

2. THE BROADER PROBLEM: THE RICH AND THE POOR IN THE WORLD

Looked at in this way we are dealing with a very practical and a very human problem which can be approached from a number of minute angles touching on how people come to feel the way they do, what makes people change their attitudes, how to put together an effective programme of education for change in attitudes and lifestyles; what kind of an atmosphere and what kind of activities should we hope to achieve in Church parishes, dioceses, presbyteries, synods, etc. This whole matter has also direct bearing on our liturgy, our homiletics, prayer and piety, and each one of these has a profound bearing on 'the whole matter' itself.

There are those who would insist that only here, in this more intimate circle—within us and in the inner circle of Christian communities and parishes—can we get at *the problem of separateness and insensitivity among the world's peoples* and hope to do anything effective about it. We would agree: we cannot ever feel at liberty to by-pass this crucial area. Further on, we want to return to it. But first it is important to look at the broader problem and broader ways of approaching it.

There is nothing accidental about the barriers and the hostility between peoples. *Power and a sense of superiority* combined with a habit of greed, normally then expressed in one form of domination or exploitation or another, produce the *separation*, which can last for centuries.

History is of course never so simple but these are classic and recurring elements. When the World Christian Community, or any local Christian community, begins inquiring after this whole matter, it is of fundamental importance to realise that behind the chief dominators and exploiters of the last two centuries (Europeans and North Americans) has been a superiority and an aggressiveness which have their *roots directly in one form of Christianity*. Europeans and North Americans—as superior bearers of the truth and persons convinced that they have been anointed to change the beliefs and the lives and status of the peoples—annexed and plundered and dominated to an extent never known before in history.

Curiously enough our look at the 'broader problem' plunges us back immediately into an embarassingly intimate problem: the possible formulation of a coherent '*confession of sins for proud and plundering Christian Nations*'. Though not very liturgical sounding, it is precisely this kind of a transmutation in our liturgy which may take place when we begin to think and speak honestly about what we are doing in the world. Something radical must happen to the Christian World, to the way in which it looks out upon—looks down upon—other worlds or else there will be no basis for the hope that a truly new relationship may be forged with those formerly and currently oppressed.

Few people in Western churches realise how much pride and, indeed, heresy is involved in our way of coming before the Lord and worshipping. We worship as individuals or as individual communities/congregations. We confess our individual shortcomings and seek healing and forgiveness with the same limited perspective. And when small minority groups, especially in the Third World, raise people's consciousness regarding historical and global sins which continue to cause great damage in the world, they are rejected as heretical.

There is a *curious ecumenical dimension* to this matter. Just as Western (Christian) religion has shown a particular tendency towards aggressiveness, *Eastern religions* have tended more to be pacific, profoundly life-respecting. Thus the soul-searching which we have found necessary among European and North American Christians before any real new steps can be taken towards a human relationship with the world's dispossessed nations may perhaps best be searched for in ecumenical dialogue with members of Eastern religions, who may alone be able to call us to the things that belong to true peace. Put more ecumenically: is it possible that 'the things that make for peace' (Luke 19:42), which Christianity has often found strange and unattractive, could only then become more discernible and accessible when searched for in open, honest, world-ecumenical dialogue with oriental religions, where peace has been classically so central?

Looking at the World with broad human and Gospel concerns means for the Church—and any other group—taking seriously in any given situation *the political alternatives*. This does not mean essentially taking sides or backing fully one part or another—although responsibility may demand precisely that at some specific historical junctures. What is essential is the full awareness of the *relationships between human welfare and power* and of the ways in which power can enhance or jeopardise human welfare.

This is true of all power but it is especially pertinent with regard to the power that we ourselves wield, whether we want to or not, just by being where we are—socially, economically, nationally—at a particular moment in history. No faithful church, anywhere in the world, can disregard this reality nor fail to assume in some caring way this responsibility. Among thinking Christians it is no longer news that *neutrality is impossible* in this area—that, in fact, one of the most 'effective' ways to play politics is by staying out of it. There is still however an important piece of work to be done among broad sectors of the Church's membership for whom political neutrality is understood to be one of the hallmarks of the Gospel.

One of the most striking things for us during our brief stay in *Nicaragua* was the sharp contrast between the situation there as painted by laymen, missionaries and clergy both Protestant and Catholic and the situation as described in the United States by both government and non-government sources. The matter is particularly serious since it has to do not just with discrepancies of information but with an undeclared regional war, already well underway, or, eventually, the initial spark of a Third World War. One must conclude that the churches of Nicaragua do not have communication with their counterparts in the United States, or that they have it but do not use it, or that they use it but the churches there do not take seriously what they hear, or that the constituencies of these churches do not believe the message. In any case the terrible tragedy is that the churches in Nicaragua—at all points of the theological spectrum—have ample experience and information for debunking the official U.S. government tale designed to justify the militarisation of the area but the story that actually gets through is the official one with little or no experience or information behind it.

Whatever else this story of *communication failure* may teach us, it is surely clear that, in addition to the Gospel itself, there are many things that the Church should tell the World, in the interest of Peace and well-being, which somehow it usually manages not to tell.

Nicaragua is a special case in point because it is immediate and dangerous, perhaps globally dangerous, but it is otherwise not particularly unusual. The awareness which the developed world has of trouble spots in the Third World comes from the news services often with enviable journalistic expertise but also an instinctive awareness of what people want to hear and what friendly governments want to say. What these sources do not have is precisely what national churches do have: long standing presence in the country in question, a multiplicity of contacts in distinct areas of society, personal awareness of current conflicting points of view. It would sound strange to say that part of the Church's mission is to become a *special news service*. But Nicaragua is not the only place where the Church might alter history in the direction of peace simply by *telling what it knows and what it sees*. Information has passed back and forth within the Church for centuries. Has the time not come to let the world in on the process?

A close friend and colleague, a Protestant pastor self-exiled from Chile to save his life 'invented' a ministry which corresponds rather closely to these concerns and convinced a Protestant denomination in the United States to hire him to carry it out. It involved full time work living in the United States making frequent extensive trips to Latin America and then speaking widely on both continents to Church groups, student groups, civic groups. There was a constantly growing demand for his interpretive speaking and a growing number of non-Church groups became interested in participating in the process of understanding what was going on in the rest of the Americas, looking precisely through the eyes of a committed churchman.

3.   ANOTHER LOOK AT THE INTIMATE

Much more space could be dedicated to *different ways of getting a hold of the macro-problem* and responding to it in the context of the Believing Church. But, as promised, we want to look again at the problem from a more intimate, parochial, angle. We have already suggested that some radical changes might take place in the usual practice of *confessing sins* if it were set in the broad context of society and history. Indeed the whole of a parish would undergo profound changes if the life of the community were located in this way. Each part of the liturgy would come to be seen as global in nature—not because we had invented it, but because we had discovered something which had always been there: the sacraments, the prayers, the homiletical fare, special liturgical gestures, special liturgies of solidarity with sister/brother communities/peoples around the world.

Precisely who learned from whom may not be clear but the practice now classical among the members of Amnesty International whereby the spouse and family of a political prisoner are adopted and cared for—even though the ties stretch halfway round the world—is a kind of human sensitivity very much in keeping with the best forms of Christian ministry. There is an urgency and humanity here which could keep Christian caring in close touch with real human problems and concretely aware of the broad political context that can bear so much weight on the degree of human suffering. And the liturgical, intellectual and practical aspects of parish life could be profoundly affected by this type of caring.

There is a deep inner relationship between this kind of *caring across the continents* and the kind of sensitivity a parish may have to human need across the street or across the city. Poverty, injustice and suffering are essentially the same wherever found in the world and it is therefore senseless to recognise it one place and not another.

One of the most imaginative attempts to deal with prejudice, segregation and poverty took place in *Pittsburgh*, Pennsylvania during the tumultuous 'racial' years of the late 60's. Two Presbyterian parishes, one White, upper middle class and in a privileged neighbourhood, the other Black, lower class and located in the inner city agreed to designate six families each who were to withdraw as members of their own church and become members of the other church. The idea was that racial understanding and acceptance was more likely to come from living, serving, worshipping and working together than from special interracial meetings or pronouncements. The programme was carried on for several years with what were recognised generally as very encouraging results. The processes learned and the sensitivities cultivated were intimately related to what is called for in understanding Latin America today, or South Africa, or Lebanon.

The Christian family is a very unique world-wide organisation. Few, if any, other organisations are as firmly rooted in as many parts of the World. And few, if any, are as deeply committed to being there, all over the world, at the same time deeply and essentially bound to the brother/sister communities elsewhere in the World. That this family should be, in all of its parts, aware and open to the World and to the broader Christian family, that it should be intelligent and truth-telling, is of fundamental importance to its own health and that of the World.

Contributors

JUAN ALFARO OSB, was born in Navarre, Spain. He joined the Benedictine Order at the Abbey of Our Lady of Montserrat in Manila, Philippines. He did his doctoral studies in theology at the University of Saint Thomas, in Manila and his Scriptural studies at the Pontifical Biblical Institute in Rome. After teaching at the Benedictine School in Manila, he went to the Mexican American Cultural Center in San Antonio, Texas, in 1983. He teaches also at the Incarnate Word College Pastoral Institute, in San Antonio, as well as in several Hispanic Pastoral Centers in the United States. He has written numerous books and articles for Hispanics in the U.S. and is a lecturer in biblical themes especially in the U.S. and Mexico.

GEORGES CASALIS was born in 1917 in Paris. He is a member of the Reformed Church of France and a theologian by profession. He has sucessively been secretary general of the Fédération franccaise des associations chrétiannes d'étudiants (1940), voluntary combattant in the resistance, pastor in the Vendée (1943), member of the ecumenical mission of reconciliation in Berlin (1945), pastor of the Lutheran church in Alsace (1950), professor of practical theology and hermeneutics at the Institut protestant de théologie (Faculté de Paris), assessor at the Bureau de la Fédération protestante de France and then president of the general commission of evangelisation of the Reformed church of France, vice-president of the Christian conference for peace (1982), administrator of the Musée Calvin de Noyon, member of the council of the CIMADE, president of the committee for the coordination of solidarity between France and Nicaragua. His recent publications include *Kénose et Histoire* (1970), *Lectures bibliques des protestants* (1970), *Prédication, acte politique* (1970), *Protestantisme* (1976) *Les Idées justes ne tombent pas du ciel* (1977) (translated into several languages), *Libération et religion*

(1981), *Luther et l'Église confessante* (1983), and numerous contributions to collective works in France and abroad.

MICHEL CLÉVENOT was born at Paris in 1932. He studied philology and theology, and was national chaplain of the JEC (Young Christian Students) in France from 1967 to 1972. He was literary director of Editions du Cerf from 1972 to 1976 and a journalist on *Politique-Hebdo* and *Monde-Dimanche* from 1976 to 1979, as well as a writer. He is the author of *Approches matérialistes de la Bible* (Paris, 1976) (Eng. trans., Orbis Books, New York) and *Les Hommes de la Fraternité* (History of Christianity), six vols already published out of a total of twelve (Paris, from 1981). He is general editor of a symposium on 'état des réligions' to appear in Paris in 1987. He contributes to the journals *Lettre, Notre Histoire* and *Autrement*.

RICHARD COUCH has been a fraternal worker with the Presbyterian Church U.S.A. in Argentina for the past 27 years. During that time he was professor of systematics and ethics at ISEDET (Protestant Higher Institute of Theological Study) in Buenos Aires until 1980 and in 1961-63 served that institution as Vice Rector and acting Rector. From 1972 to 1980 he served as Director of the Christian Study Center, Buenos Aires. He is currently theological secretary in the Institute for Ecumenical Relations (IRE), Buenos Aires and coordinator of a special ecumenical project for liturgical renewal under the auspices of the Ecumenical Center in Montevideo, Uruguay. Dr. Couch's basic theological study was done in Princeton Theological Seminary. Special graduate studies were done in Union Theological Seminary, New York, and the theological faculties in Bonn and Strasbourg. His publications include *Familia y Sociedad* (Buenos Aires) co-authored with group of River Plate scholars and professionals, and an article on the biblical concept of conscience in *Testimonium* a review, published by Student Christian Movement in Argentina (MEC).

ENRIQUE DUSSEL is an Argentine and a Catholic and lives in Mexico. He holds doctorates in philosophy (Madrid 1959) and history (Sorbonne 1967) and an honorary doctorate in theology (Freiburg 1981). He is professor of ethics in the Autonomous University of Mexico and of Church history and theological method in ITES (Mexico). He is president of the Church history commission (CEHILA) and coordinator of the same commission in EA-TWOT (the Ecumenical Association of Third World Theologians). Among his writings are *A History of the Church in Latin America* (1981); *Philosophy of Liberation* (1985); *Etica comunitaria* ('Community Ethics'), in the collection 'Theology and Liberation' (1986) (English, German and French translations in preparation).

WALTER FERNANDES SJ, a jesuit priest and a sociologist, is director of the Indian Social Institute, New Delhi and editor of *Social Action*. He has written over a dozen books and many other papers on people's participation in development, environment and tribals and the Indian Catholic Community. Some of his main works are: *Caste and Conversion Movements in India* (1981); *Participatory Research and Evaluation: Experiments in Research as a Process of Liberation* (1981); *Towards a New Forest Policy: People's Rights and Environmental Needs* (1983); *Forests, Environment and People: Ecological Values and Social Costs* (1983); *Trade Unions and Industrial Relations in India* (1984); *Social Activists and People's Movements: Search for Political and Economic Alternatives* (1985); *Inequality, Its Bases and Search for Solutions* (1986).

DAVID FLOOD UFM, born in Biddeford, Maine, in 1929, entered the Franciscan order in 1950. He studied Franciscan history with Kajetan Esser, helping him in 1970-1971 with the critical edition of the early Franciscan writings (*Opuscula Sancti Patris Francisci Assisiensis*, Grottaferrata, 1978: The writings of Our Holy Father Francis). In the 1980s he has published articles on Franciscan history in *Franziskanische studien* and *Wissenschaft und Weisheit*, as well as *Frère Franccois et le mouvement franciscain* (1983). At present he lives in Möchengladbach, West Germany.

NORBERT GREINACHER is Professor of Practical Theology at the University of Tübingen, and has published many books on the pastoral and social aspects of Christian faith, including: *Soziologie der Pfarrei* (1955); *Angst in der Kirche verstehen und überwinden* (1972); *Christliche Rechtfertigung—Gesellschaftliche Gerechtigkeit* (1973); *Einführung in die praktische Theologie* (1976); *Gelassene Leidenschaft* (1977); *Gemeindepraxis. Analysen und Aufgaben* (1979); *Der Fall Küng. Eine Dokumentation* (1980); *Freiheitsrechte für Christen?* (1980); *Christsein als Beruf* (1981); *Im Angesicht meiner Feinde—Mahl des Friedens* (1982); *El Salvador—Massaker im Namen der Freiheit* (1982); *Der Konflikt um die Theologie der Befreiung* (1985); *Kirche der Armen. Sur Theologie der Befreiung* (1985); *Umkehr und Neubeginn* (1986); *Katholische Kirche—Wohin?* (with H. Küng [ed.] 1986); *Menschlich leben* (1986); *Der Schrei nach Gerechtigkeit* (1986).

RAINER KAMPLING was born in Neuenkirchen, Münsterland, in 1953.

After doing community service he studied theology, Latin philology and Judaism. After gaining his doctorate in theology, he joined the teaching staff of the Catholic Faculty of theology of the university of Paderborn. His publications include *Das Blut Christi und die Juden. Mt. 27:25 bei den lateinnischsprachigen christlichen Autoren bis zu Leo dem Grossen* (1984) and various contributions to New Testament themes and the history of the early Church.

JOHN KAVANAUGH SJ was ordained a priest in the Society of Jesus, June 1971. He gained the degrees of Master of Arts, Licentiate in Philosophy, Master in Divinity and Master in Dogmatic Theology at Saint Louis University (1965-71) and a doctorate in social philosophy at Washington University in 1973. He is a syndicated columnist in Catholic newspapers through the *Saint Louis Review*. He was awarded United States National Catholic Press Awards in social commentary for 1978 and 1984. He is the author of *Following Christ in a Consumer Society* (1981) and *Human Realization* (1970). He lectures on the topics of Consumerism, American Culture, Poverty, Community Life, and the Spirituality of Cultural Resistance. He has given presentations and workshops in the United States and Canada, South and Central America, Europe. His areas of specialisation in teaching on the university level are philosophies of human identity and action, social philosophy, Thomism, Marxism, Freud. His international experience includes six months in India (with tenures at the Missionaries of Charity in Calcutta and the Jean Vanier communities for the handicapped in Bangalore and Madras). He spent eight years as the Missouri Province (Society of Jesus) Assistant for Social Justice.

SAMUEL RAYAN SJ was born in 1920, entered the Society of Jesus in 1939, and was ordained priest in 1955. He gained a degree in literature in 1950 in the university of Trivandrum and a doctorate in theology in 1960 at the Gregorian University, Rome. He was chaplain to the University Students Organisation in Kerala, 1961-1972 and has been Professor of theology at the VidyaJyoti, Delhi, since 1972. He served as a member on the WCC Commission on Faith and Order, 1968-1982. He is sectional editor of *Jeevadhara*, a journal of theology. He has contributed articles to periodicals in India and abroad. His publications include: *The Holy Spirit* (1978); *The Anger of God* (1982).

JULIO DE SANTA ANA was born in Montevideo in 1934. He studied theology in Buenos Aires and took a doctorate in Religious Sciences at Strasbourg in 1962. From 1963 he held various posts in the ecumenical movement in South America, and was Director of the Department for Cultural Expansion at Montevideo University in 1972. Having to leave Uruguay for political reasons, he worked for the World Council of Churches, becoming Director of its Commission for Church Participation in Development from 1979-82. He is now co-Director of the Ecumenical Centre for Evangelisation and Popular Education in São Paulo. He has published books on Christianity without Religion, Protestantism, Culture and Society in Latin America, The Way of the Kingdom and *Good News to the Poor.*

Theology, Church and Ministry

John Macquarrie

A new collection of essays. Topics covered include 'Pilgrimage in Theology', 'The Idea of a People of God', 'Pride in the Church', 'Politics as Lay Ministry' and 'The Ordination of Women to the Priesthood'. John Macquarrie retires this summer as Lady Margaret Professor of Divinity in the University of Oxford.

£6.95   *paper*

Provisional Churches

Christian Duquoc

The many different churches have, by and large, come to accept each other's existence. Professor Duquoc argues that this multiplicity is the starting point for a new ecclesiology that accepts the churches as provisional, and so encourages ecumenical unity.

£4.95   *paper*

Understanding Karl Rahner

Herbert Vorgrimler

An introduction to the work of Karl Rahner that demonstrates that Rahner's writings are not as unapproachable as they are made out to be. This book puts the man and his writings in context and provides encouragement to read the works of Rahner for yourself.

£5.95   *paper*

The Two Catholic Churches

A Study in Opression

Catholicism in England is associated with traditional working class, predominantly Irish, communities, but now also with 'trendy' radicals who are middle class, affluent, pro-Vatican II and admirers of Schillebeeckx, Kung and others. Neither group is really in line with current Vatican teaching. What is the future for the Catholic church in England, and can the gap between official Catholicism and Catholicism as it actually exists be bridged?

£8.50   *limp*

So Near and Yet So Far

Rome, Canterbury and ARCIC

Hugh Montefiore

An attempt to put in perspective for the ordinary church-goer the achievements of the Anglican-Roman Catholic International Commission. Though not over impressed with progress on doctrinal agreement, Bishop Montefiore stresses that at the 'grass roots', changes are being made and prejudices shed as communities work more and more closely together.

£5.95   *paper*

SCM Press Ltd
26-30 Tottenham Road
London N1 4BZ

Jesus Christ Liberator
A Critical Christology of Our Time
Leonard Boff

In Jesus Christ Liberator Leonard Boff reveals his views on the life, message and practical activity of Jesus. It is liberation, not only from personal sin, but also from the sins of society – poverty, injustice and oppression. **£7.50**

All You Love is Need
Tony Walter

'Tony Walter gives an admirably documented analysis and powerful critique of the loose thinking in the Western world centred on the concept of Need . . . Here is a clear and closely reasoned challenge.' – *Expository Times*

'A book which is worthy of much serious consideration' – *Baptist Times*

'What he has to say is valuable and provocative . . . this is a book well worth buying, particularly if you need to have your comfortable assumptions overturned.' – *Church of England Newspaper*

A Third Way Book   **£3.95**

Transforming Economics
Alan Storkey

Although unemployment dominates political and church discussions, there is no theological basis for the churches' concern. This book will end this by examining critically the traditional economic theories and presenting an alternative Christian approach to economics. It examines the central Christian response to unemployment through a range of policies which suggest a new way of tackling the problem.

A Third Way Book   **£5.95**

CONVERSATIONS ON COUNSELLING

Edited by Marcus Lefébure

Conversations on Counselling offers a deeply experienced and thought out spiritual interpretation of counselling work drawing on personal case-work and references to Aquinas, Augustine, Buddha, Jung and Rudolf Steiner.

> "[Conversations on Counselling] is short, well written and invaluable and should be read by everybody who is concerned about human relationships and is actually doing counselling work."
>
> *Dr. Jack Dominian, Consultant Psychiatrist*

Paperback   £4.95

HUMAN EXPERIENCE AND THE ART OF COUNSELLING

Edited by Marcus Lefébure

A sequel to the widely read *Conversations on Counselling*, the main theme is that although counselling does involve certain professional technical skills, it remains an art which should be firmly grounded in concern, common sense, and humanity.

Paperback   £4.95

T & T Clark Ltd
59 George Street, Edinburgh EH2 2LQ, Scotland

CONCILIUM

CONCILIUM

CONCILIUM 1985

All back issues are still in print: available from bookshops (price £3.95) or direct from the publisher (£4.45/US$7.70/Can$8.70 including postage and packing).

T. & T. CLARK LTD, 59 GEORGE STREET, EDINBURGH EH2 2LQ, SCOTLAND